I0729592

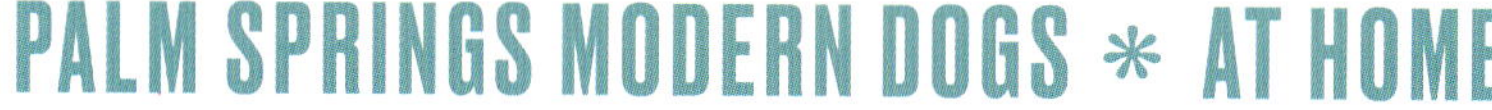
PALM SPRINGS MODERN DOGS * AT HOME

Book design by Nancy Baron and Kali Malinka
Cover design by Rex Bonomelli
Photographs and text copyright ©Nancy Baron 2019
Photograph of Sia's pets copyright ©Sia 2019
Type set in Druk/Univers
ISBN: 978-0-7643-5996-5
Printed in India
5 4 3 2

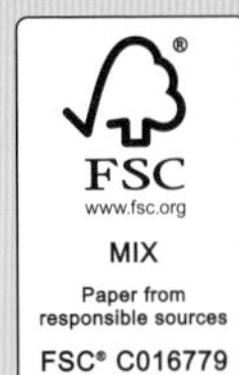

Published by Schiffer Publishing, Ltd.
4880 Lower Valley Road
Atglen, PA 19310
Phone: (610) 593-1777; Fax: (610) 593-2002
E-mail: Info@schifferbooks.com
Web: www.schifferbooks.com

NANCY BARON

PALM SPRINGS MODERN DOGS * AT HOME

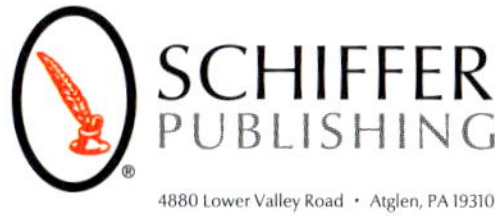

SCHIFFER PUBLISHING

4880 Lower Valley Road • Atglen, PA 19310

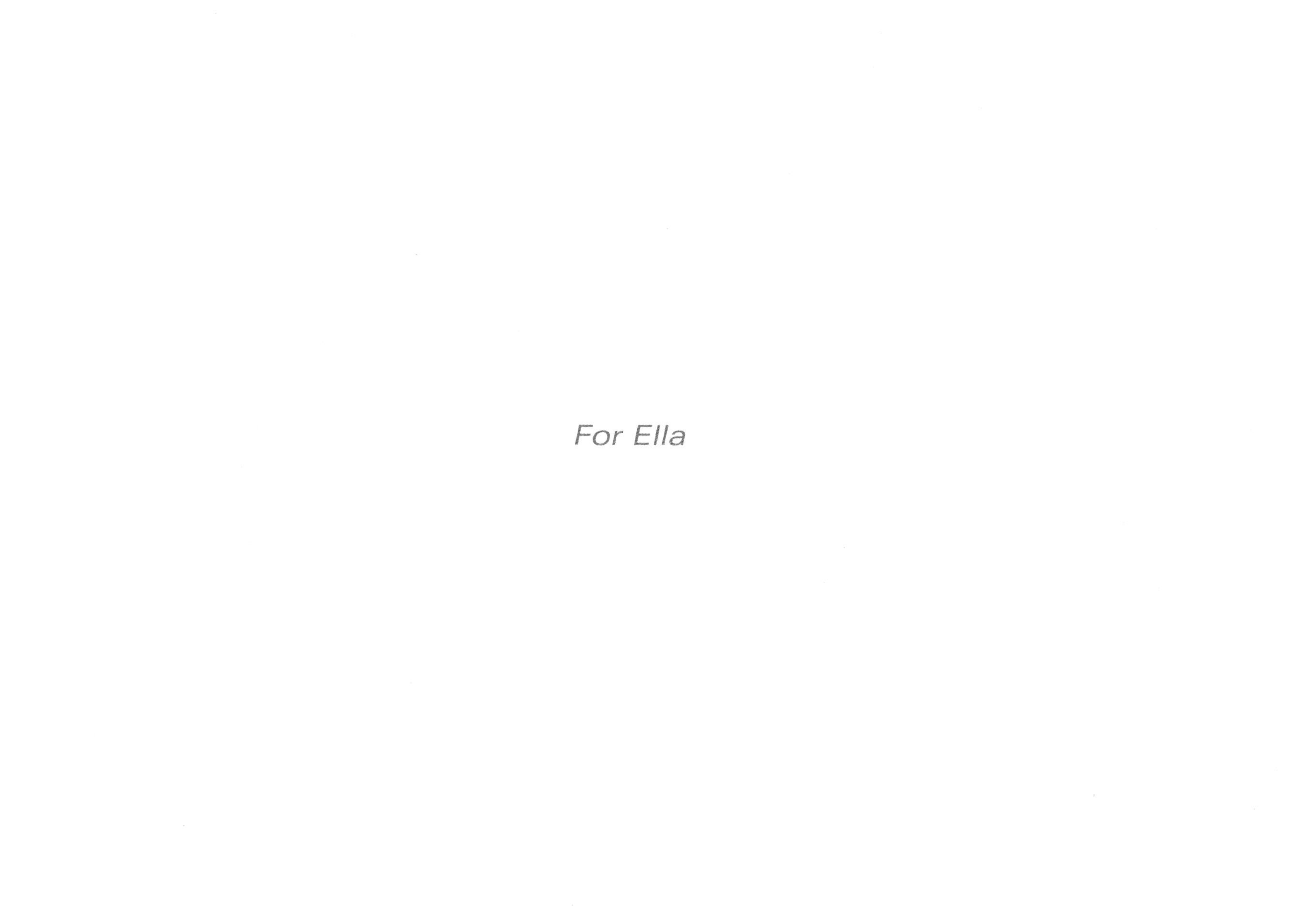

For Ella

I smell like dogs.

I love dogs.

I have dogs. I got dogs.

I am a dog lover.

I'm a dog lady dogging it up.

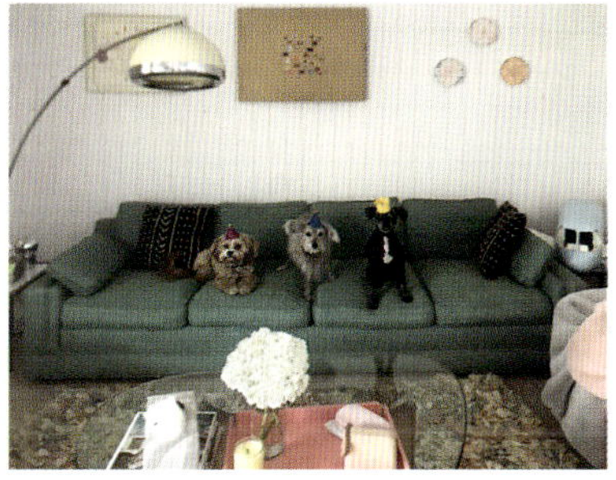

quote and photo

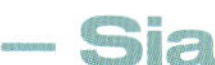

— Sia

Foreword

In her third book, focused, pun intended, on Palm Springs living, Nancy Baron's keen eye looks at the role that dogs play—and run and jump and fetch—in making the town the singular place it is. Topography, climate, and architecture have certainly played their parts in creating a setting that is world renowned. Yet, the town's *Modern Dogs*—from Chihuahuas to wolfhounds, purebreds, and rescues alike—bring it all to life. In "The Springs," that which is fun is always that much more enjoyable and fulfilling when one or more dogs are part of the mix.

Palm Springs is a special place where modernist architecture and design are curated, celebrated, and championed in no uncertain terms. The "look" of things, in that dramatic desert context, takes on added significance, but not in a facile way. Typically, the emphasis is more about one's personal style than what one earns or spends or happens to look like. Trappings of that style include, of course, one's house and decor there within. Clothes, though often minimal, thanks to the weather, offer a way to add color and verve. So, too, might a vintage car—all making for a mise-en-scène that has one questioning reality. Think the "Jet Set" episode of Mad Men, where Don Draper alights in Palm Springs and finds it difficult to discern what is real and what is not.

It's often said that dogs are a reflection of their owners' personalities and look. While most of our fellow Palm Springs residents don't (at least not that I know of) have tails, floppy ears, or cold, wet noses, their dogs are an extension of the modernist ethos, and there's a canine throughline from the town's golden era (1940s–1980s). Hollywood stars, and regular Joes alike, brought their dogs to town, and that's still very much the case. Dogs, paradoxically, humanize design in a very real way. On the street, on hiking mountain trails, in midcentury modern homes, or hanging out the window of a 1957 Plymouth Fury, the modern dog provides warmth and enthusiasm to those respective settings. More importantly, they radiate love in a town founded on the notion that we should be free to be ourselves.

Dogs help socialize their owners and provide a sense of what real life, both in the past and the current day, has to offer. They provide warmth and, with real heart and soul, underscore the humanist philosophy of modernist design.

For the most part, our fellow residents don't really care where you went to school, your station in life, or how much money you have, but, rather, if you live life with a sense of style that can be shared with and appreciated by others. In this context, dogs provide a common focus verging on obsession. The palatial Palm Springs Animal Shelter is testimony to the town's priority to make dogs, and all pets, part of that which Nancy celebrates in her book series *The Good Life* (Kehrer Verlag). Thank dog(s) for that.

Bob Merlis
Palm Springs, April 9, 2019

In good times and bad, our best friends are there for support, therapy, and unconditional love. Especially now—where would we be without our dogs? Although the so-called modernists of Palm Springs embrace the serenity of life in post–WWII America, the sometimes-harsh realities of contemporary life are impossible to ignore. These mid-twentieth century re-enactors are often transplants, enjoying the Palm Springs lifestyle with their dogs and friends as their chosen family. The beautiful climate, wide-open spaces, and clean décor make the perfect home for their desert pets that are as lovingly groomed and cared-for as their surroundings.

For the many years that Palm Springs has been my second home I've been documenting the endlessly intriguing lifestyle beyond its resorts. The community has welcomed my camera and me into their homes which are perfect odes to mid century modern American design. The dogs of the house often follow me around and wander into my camera frame, adding warmth and life to the image as they do to their homes. In these pages I have put these precious pups in the spotlight where they belong.

Nancy Baron

Ella

ENGLISH SHEPHERD

ARCHITECTS: DONALD WEXLER / RICHARD HARRISON, 1959

This youthful senior adds another warm and beating heart to our light-filled, modern home. Ella is a friend to all, and her calm energy fits right in with the zen Palm Springs vibe that offers the perfect respite from our busy LA lives. With beautiful blue skies, some of the nicest people in the US, stunning desert landscapes, and the mystical energy of the hot springs running underground, this little town is nothing less than magical.

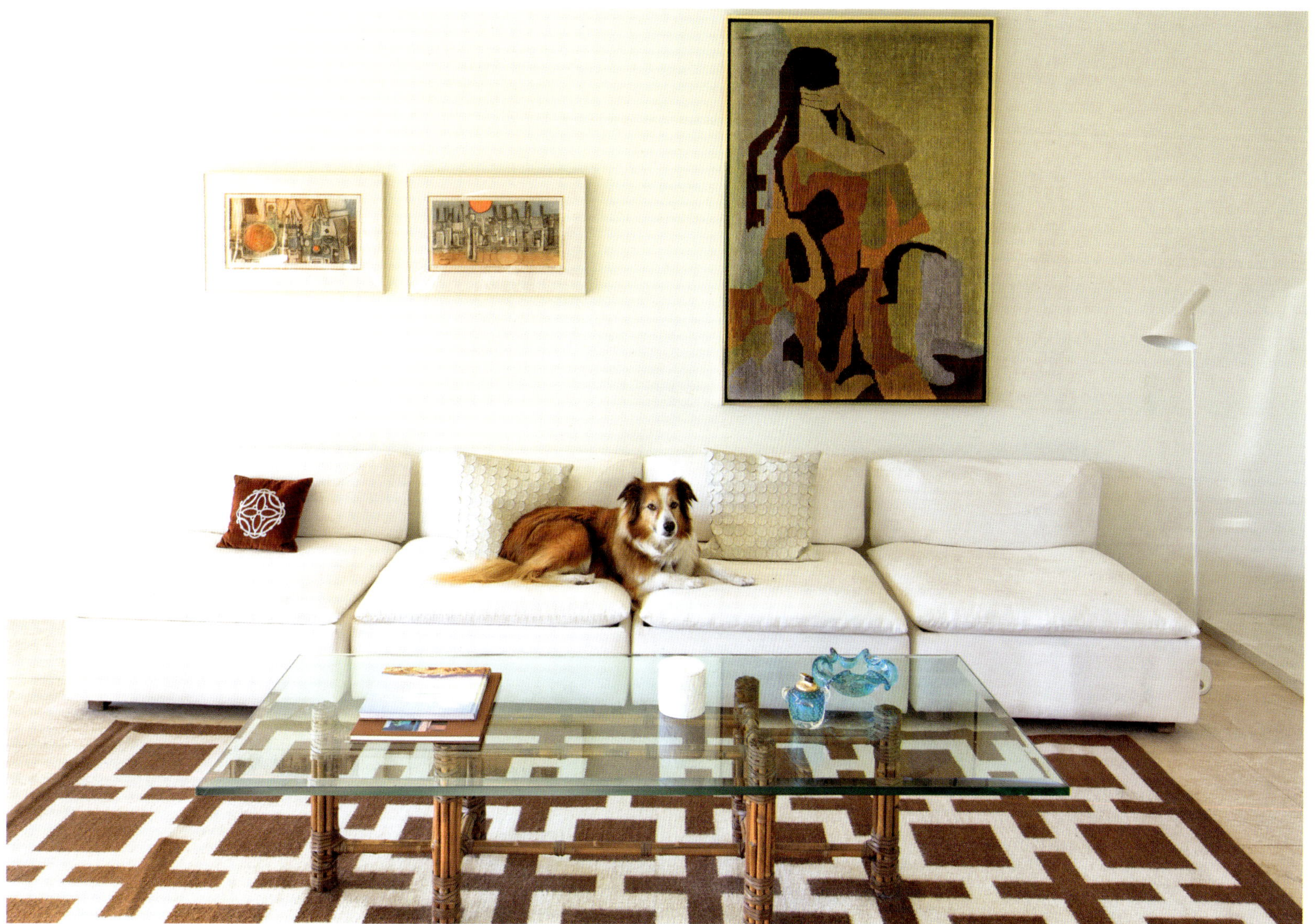

Winston and Peanut (under the table)

**SMOOTH FOX TERRIER, BORDER TERRIER
RESCUES**

ARCHITECT: DONALD WEXLER, 1965

We've always had a pair of dogs in the house. We enjoy watching them interact with each other and how they express their individual personalities. They've always been lovable and loyal.

We love the way the sun comes into the house throughout the year. Our favorite thing is opening every window and door, letting the sun and breeze carry through every room.

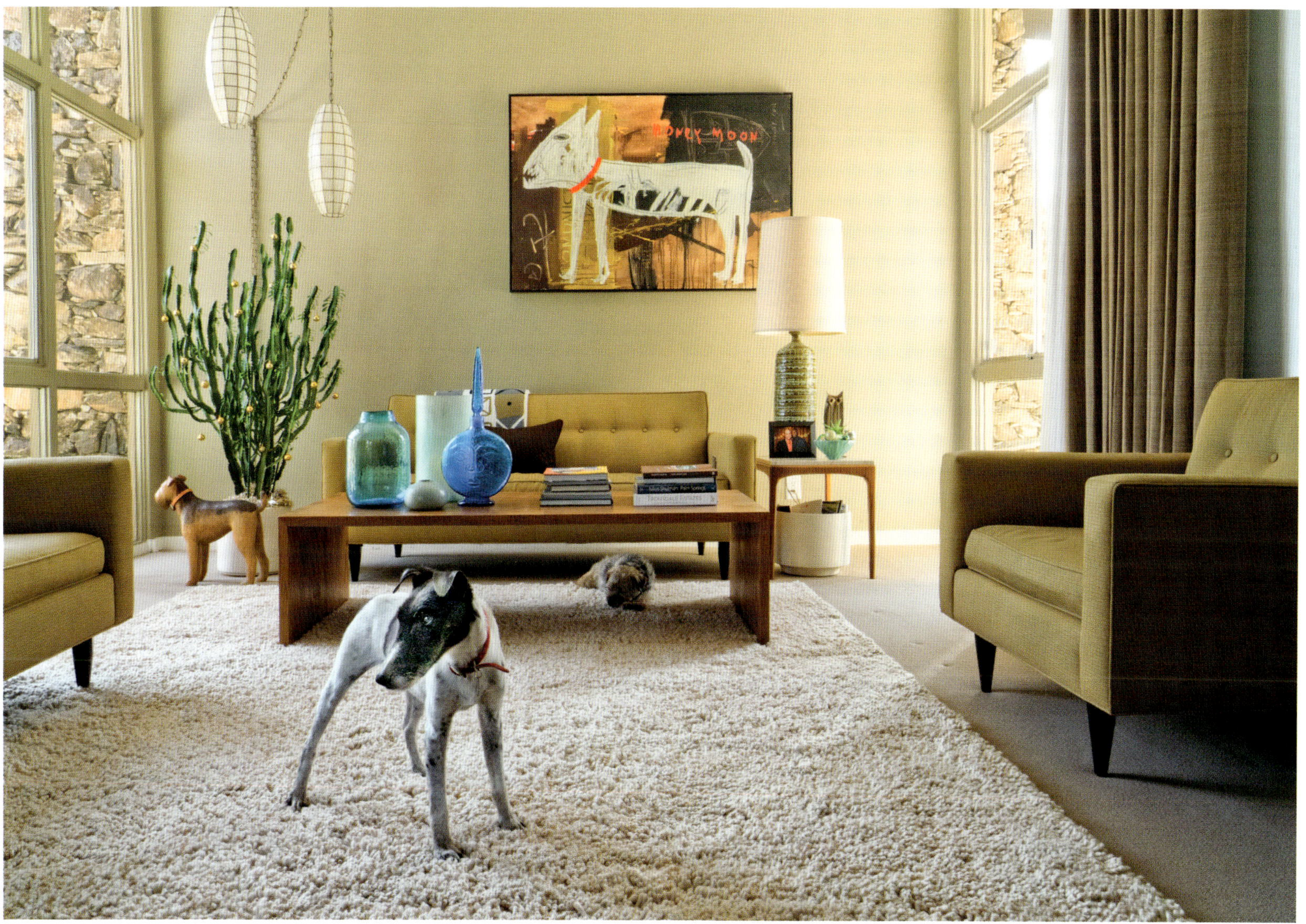

Happy

**POINTER / PIT MIX
RESCUE**

ARCHITECT: DONALD WEXLER, 1962

They don't call them man's best friend for nothing. There's nothing like the pure unconditional love of a dog's companionship.

Don Wexler came as close as anyone to realizing the modernist dream of factory-built homes. Even after twenty years, I enjoy waking up every day to the beautiful, clean logic of his design.

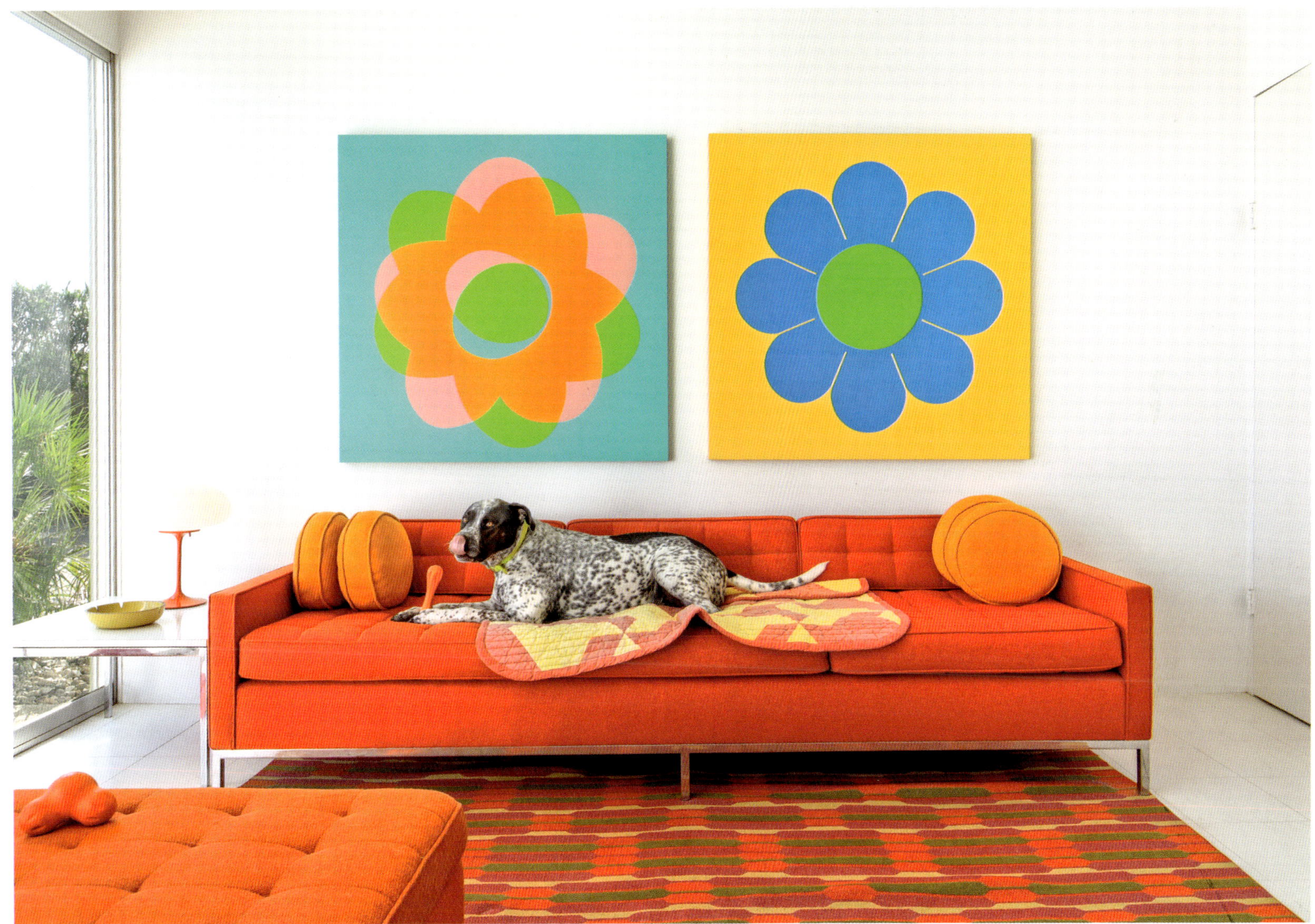

Brick

BOSTON TERRIER

ARCHITECT: WILLIAM KRISEL, 1956

I live alone with Brick, so he brings life and warmth to my home, and I could not imagine being here without him. The architecture and the look of the house are amazing, but he makes it a home.

I love the seamlessness of the interior and exterior of the home, and how happy the architecture makes you feel when you are inside but also constantly aware of Mother Nature outside. Being in the house and in Palm Springs is a tonic for the soul.

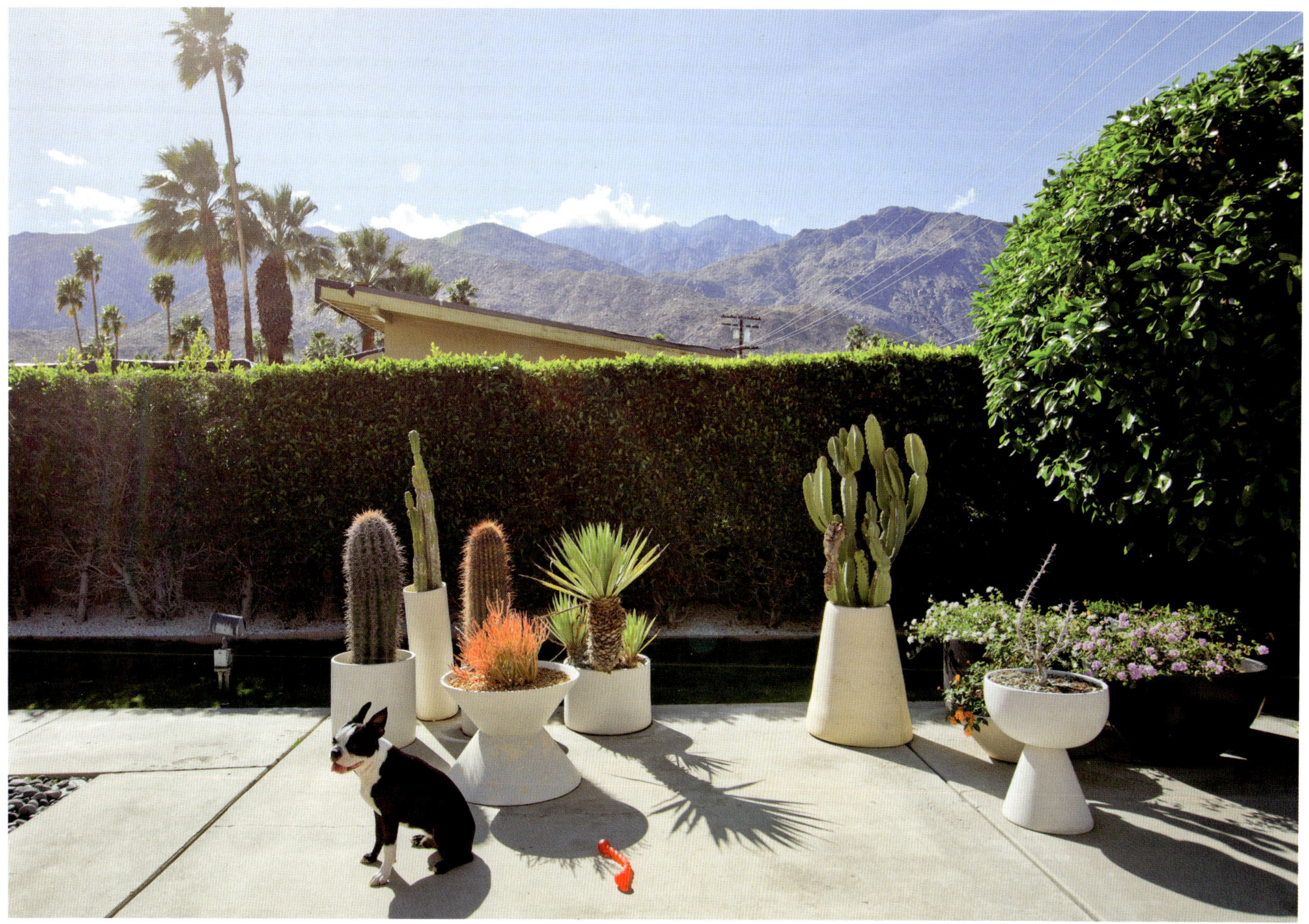

George

GOLDEN DOODLE

BUILDER: THE KARLISA COMPANY, 1959

George is a constant joy at our Palm Springs house. He uses the pool every day when we are there, and loves being able to wander in and out of the house on his own. We leave the doors open most of the time for him.

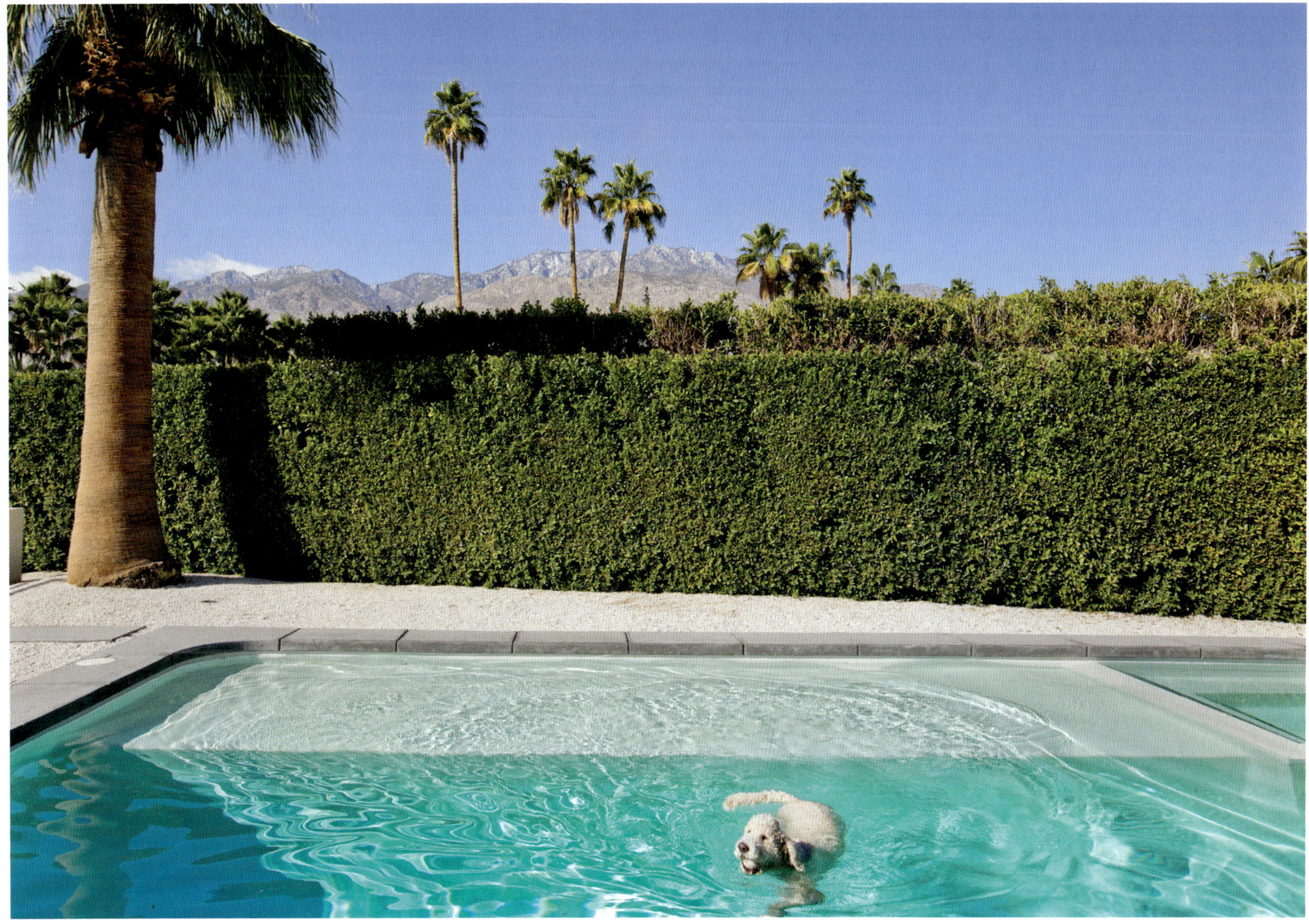

Lillian (L) and Rena

**AUSTRALIAN CATTLE DOG, BLACK LABRADOR RETRIEVER
RESCUES**

**ARCHITECT: JACK MEISELMAN, 1957
CAR: 1963 CORVAIR MONZA**

Lillian (left) and Rena are a big part of our lives. Besides riding in our vintage convertible Corvair, or just lying in the sun, they bring happiness to everyone.

We love Palm Springs. The warmth of the desert sun and the view of the mountains are why we came here.

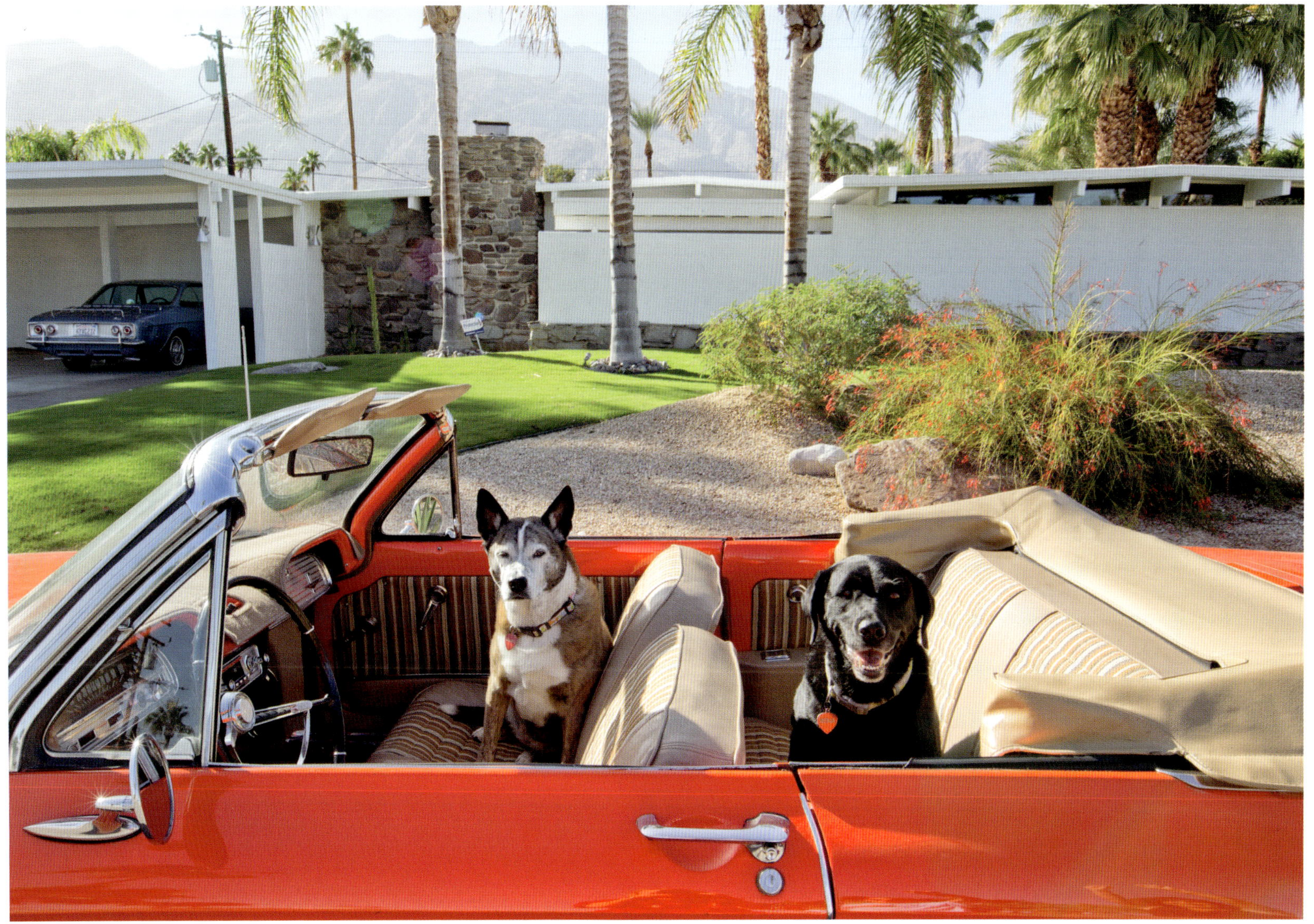

Matilda Applebaum (L) and Wyatt Bohanon

**CHIHUAHUAS
RESCUES**

ARCHITECT: JOHN LAUTNER, 1947

Our fur babies are our everything! Since we work from home, we get to spend mostly every day together. They lift up our spirits and fill our hearts. They are our true companions.

The Lautner property is integral to our lives. It was the catalyst that brought us both to the beautiful desert (and kept us here). We met and fell in love at the property. Its distinctive architecture and innovative design continue to inspire us everyday.

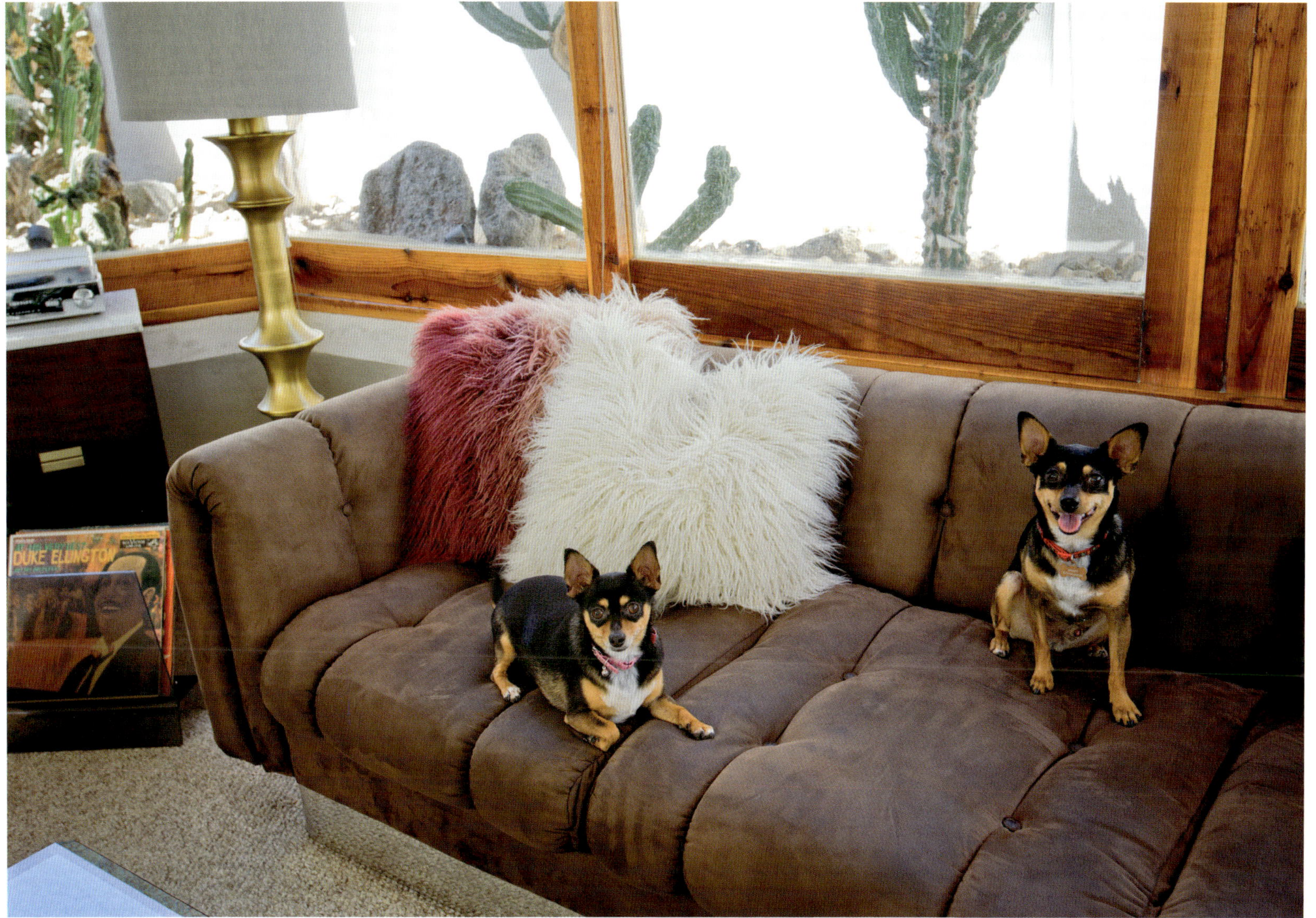
DUKE ELLINGTON

Jimmy

**JACK RUSSELL / SHIH TZU MIX
RESCUE**

ARCHITECT: DONALD WEXLER, 1960

It is impossible not to smile when Jimmy is around. If we are having a stressful day, Jimmy knows how to calm us down. He brings so much joy to our everyday lives by just being present.

We live in New York City for half of the year, so coming out to Palm Springs feels like a vacation every day. From the gorgeous weather to the picturesque views, there is nowhere else like this city. We love living in El Rancho Vista Estates. The neighborhood is full of midcentury modern enthusiasts who take great pride in their homes.

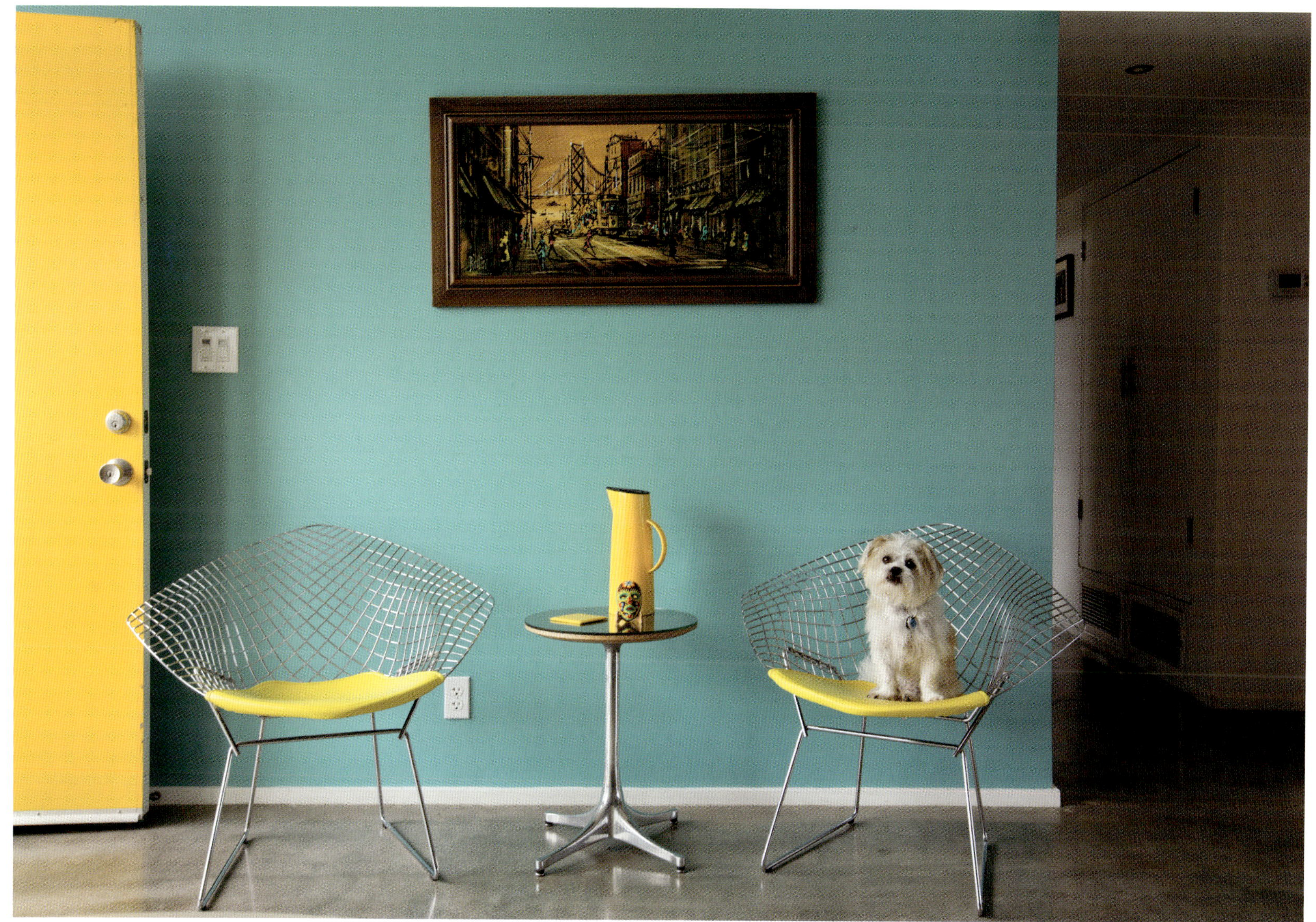

LuLu (L) and Farley

**MIXED BREEDS
RESCUES**

ARCHITECT: STAN SACKLEY, 1965

They bring spirit and life to our home! Otherwise—just a couple of guys living in a white box (lol)!

We love the light, the colorful history, and the architecture of Palm Springs.

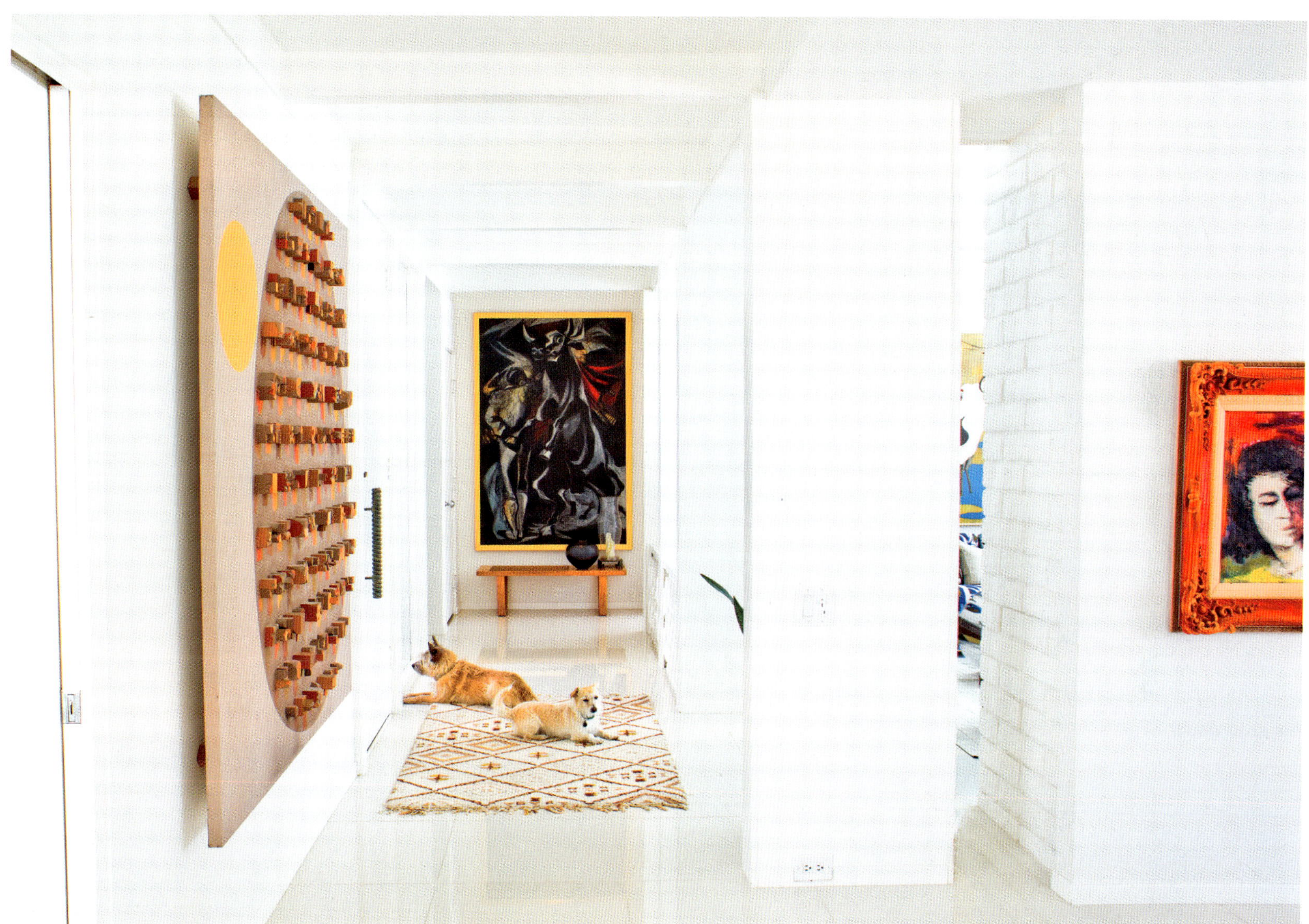

Abbey

ENGLISH SETTER

DEVELOPER: PAUL TROUSDALE, 1948

Abbey has always been a part of our family. There's that unwavering and solid bond after raising a puppy, and "who knows who best," that brings an unlimited amount of joy to our lives. Now during year five, we've watched our baby grow into a marvelous adult. She probably takes care of us as much as we do for her. Abbey is the third English setter we've raised. Each dog has had their own personality, but Abbey is probably the most loving of them all, making it easy to see why English setters are outstanding service and therapy dogs.

Even though our house was built in 1948, on the early side of the MCM movement, the Trousdale homes were built with a modern touch and are just perfect for Palm Springs. Our floor plan and the positioning of the house on our lot take advantage of full and unobstructed views of the mountains and Mt. San Jacinto. We wouldn't have it any other way. The mountains change color from sunrise to sunset all year round, and that little bit of snow on the peaks during the winter transforms them into a distant visual wonderland. Obviously, we love Palm Springs weather, being able to take advantage of our pool and yard most of the year, and the simple and easy indoor-outdoor living, which is really hard to find in most places around the country.

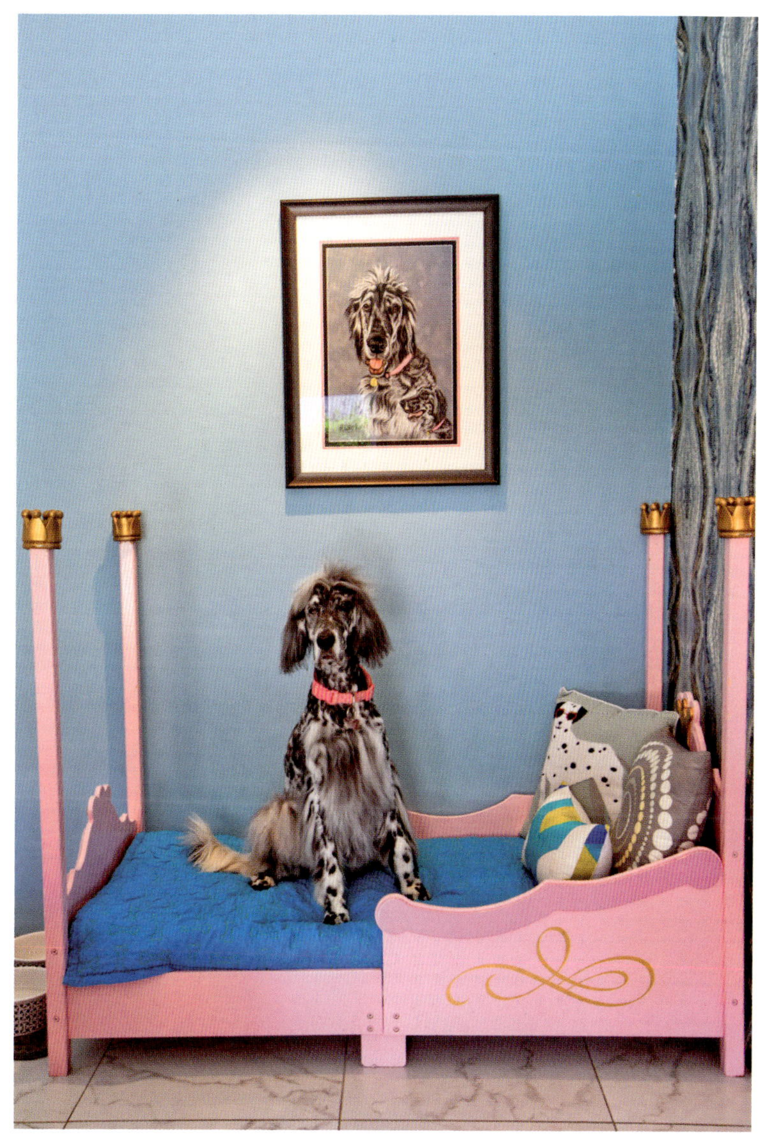

Mingus

**AUSTRALIAN SHEPHERD / CATAHOULA LEOPARD DOG MIX
RESCUE**

ARCHITECTS: ALBERT FREY AND ROBSON CHAMBERS, 1964

Mingus is a unique creature. He is a never-ending source of laughter, love, silly faces, cuddles, support, and surprise. He is my family, my friend, my cherished.

Palm Springs represents the epitome of timeless style—a blend of midcentury modern architecture, natural beauty, classic elegance, and good times. It is the good life.

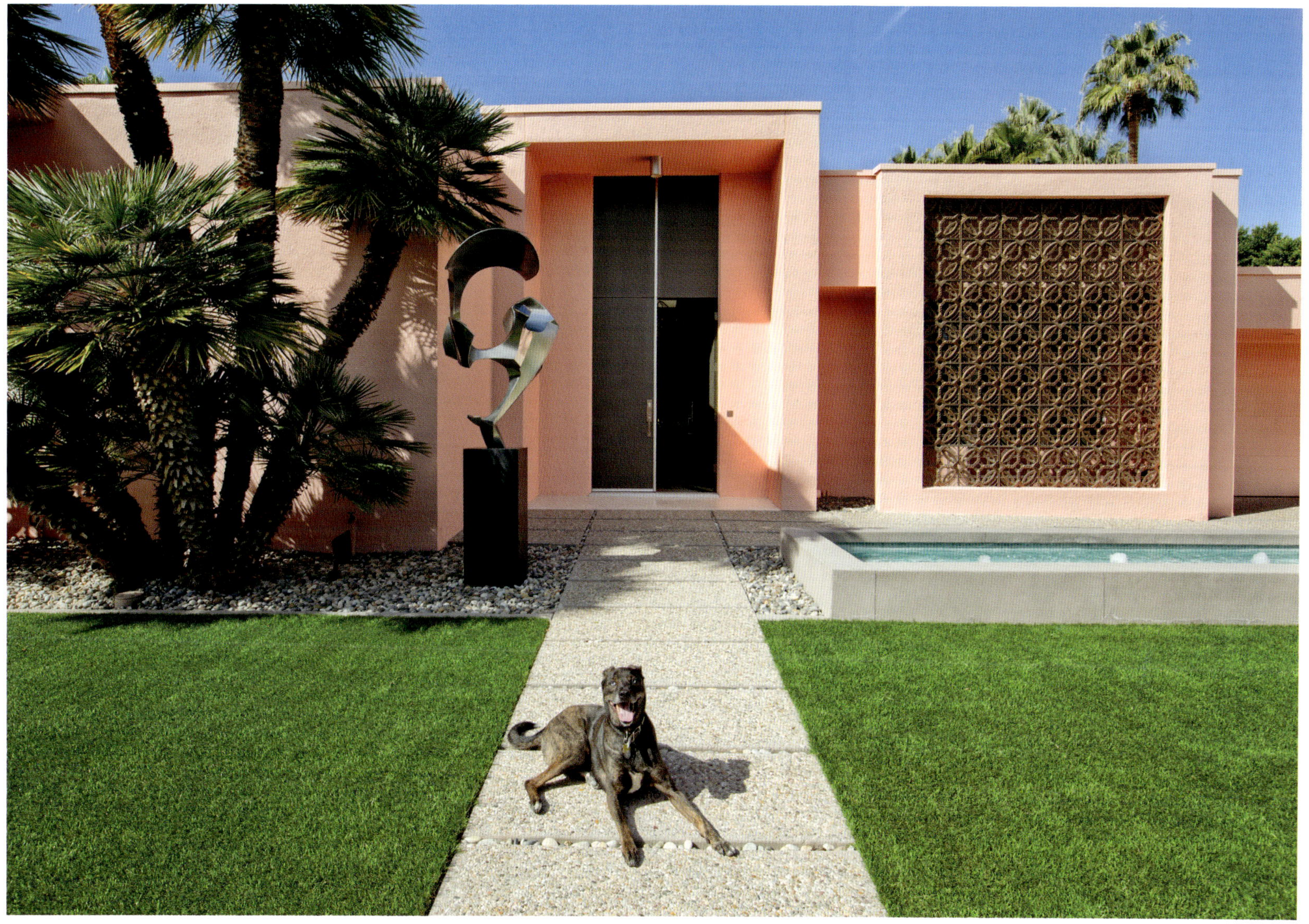

Arthur

MINIATURE DACHSHUND

ARCHITECT: DONALD WEXLER, 1960

We moved from the cold blustery winters of Chicago four years ago and have not looked back. Lola (see p. 110) and Arthur much prefer lounging in the winter sun to the quick snow-filled walks in Chicago. Seeing them be able to enjoy the outdoors year-round really brings a smile to our faces!

The MCM vibe is so relaxed and laid back. When we came to Palm Springs for vacation four years ago, we both fell in love with the natural beauty and laid-back lifestyle, so we packed up and made the trek cross country to the MCM Mecca of the US.

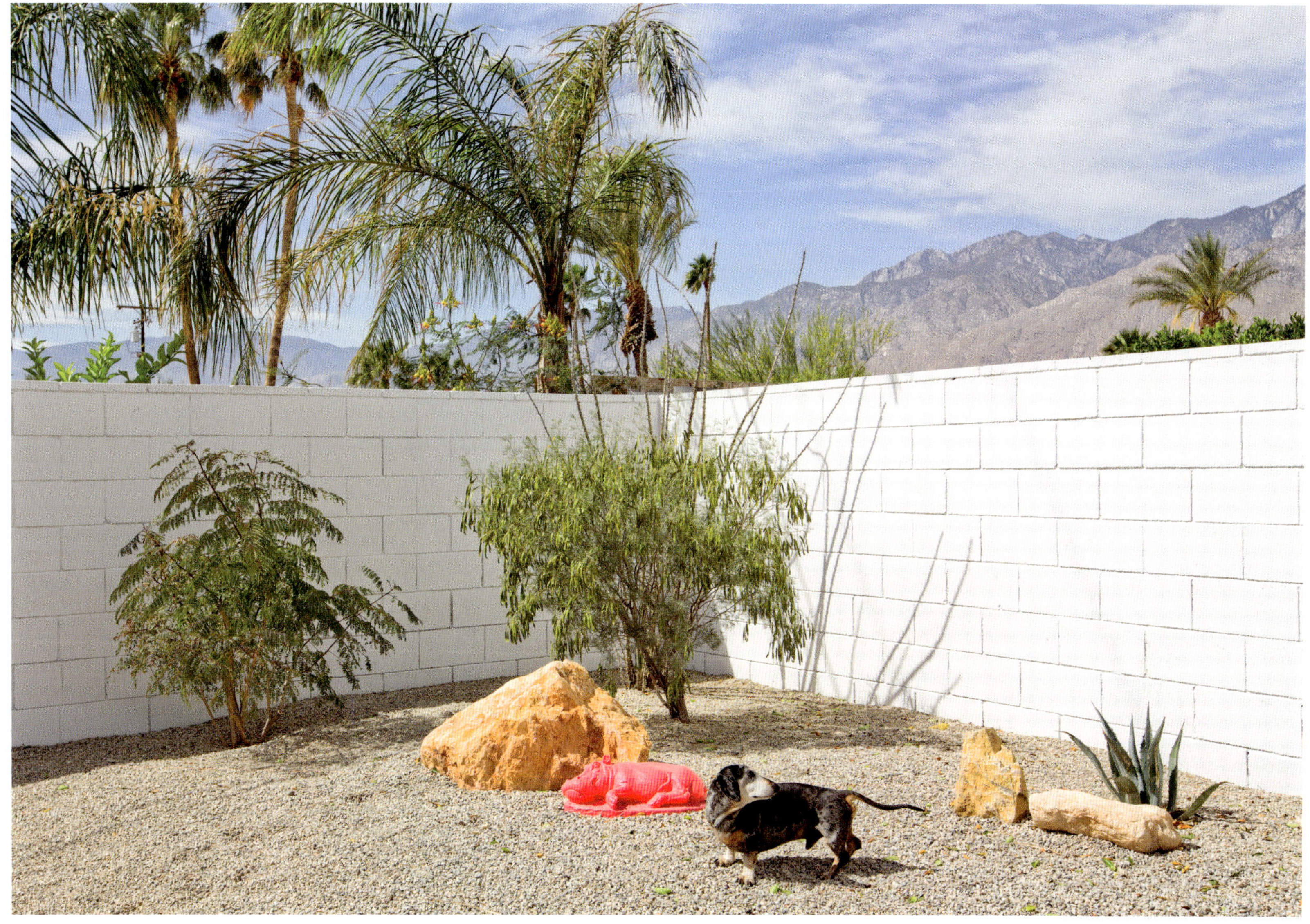

Cooper

BASSET HOUND

HOME BUILT IN 1946, EXTENSIVELY REMODELED 2013–2016

We love our basset and our beautiful and tranquil Palm Springs home.

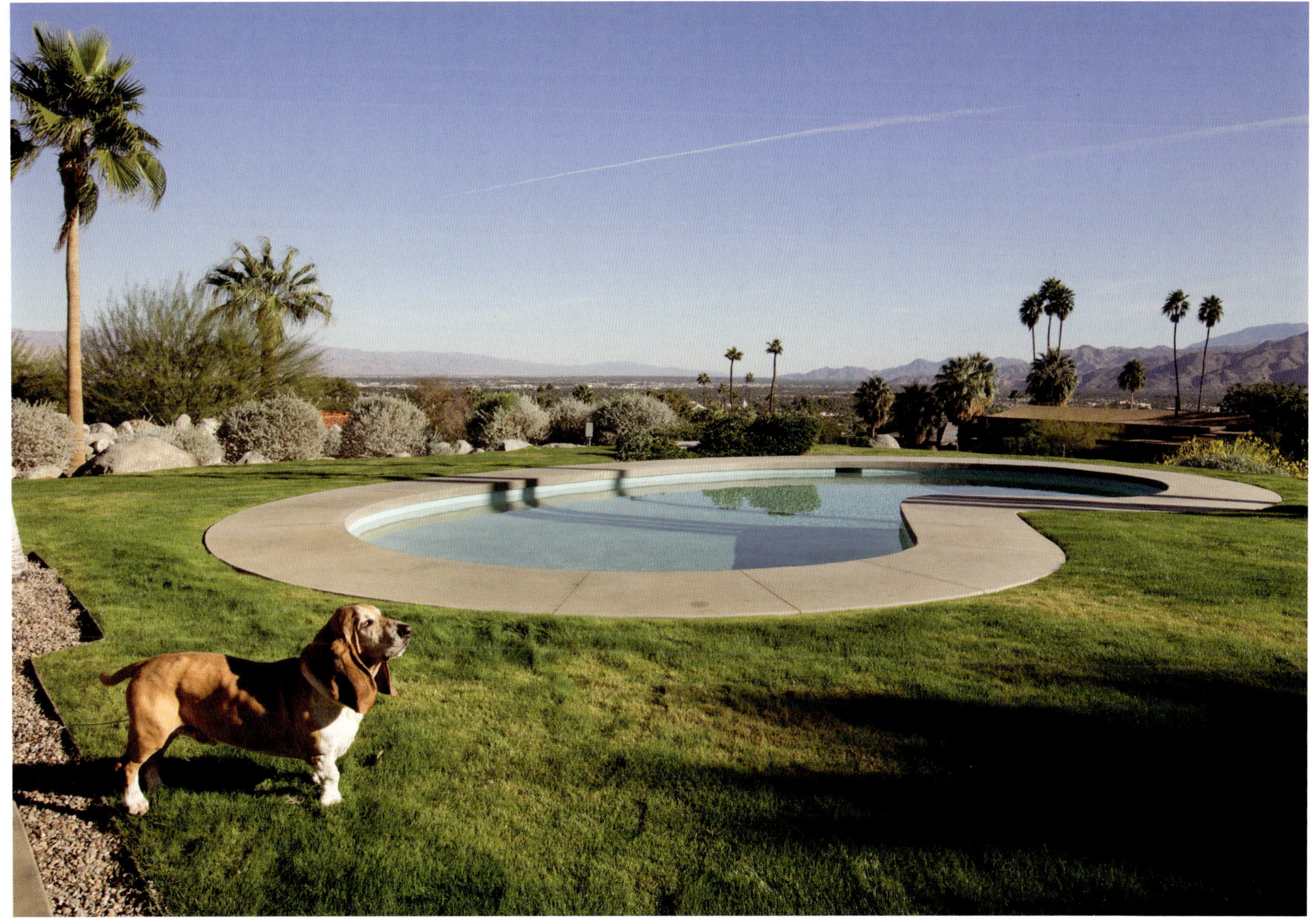

Fido Galore

**PIT MIX
RESCUE**

ARCHITECT: WILLIAM KRISEL, 1969

Fido brings our terrazzo floors to life with activity and happiness. She very much enjoys her job surveying the perimeter, keeping us apprised of all possible rabbits, deliveries, and other dogs.

We love the beauty and serenity of the California desert and the fantastically sophisticated community of Palm Springs. Each morning and evening our great joy is walking with Fido through our spectacular neighborhood of breathtakingly stunning and glamorous midcentury residences in the shadow of the great San Jacinto Mountains. Dreams do come true.

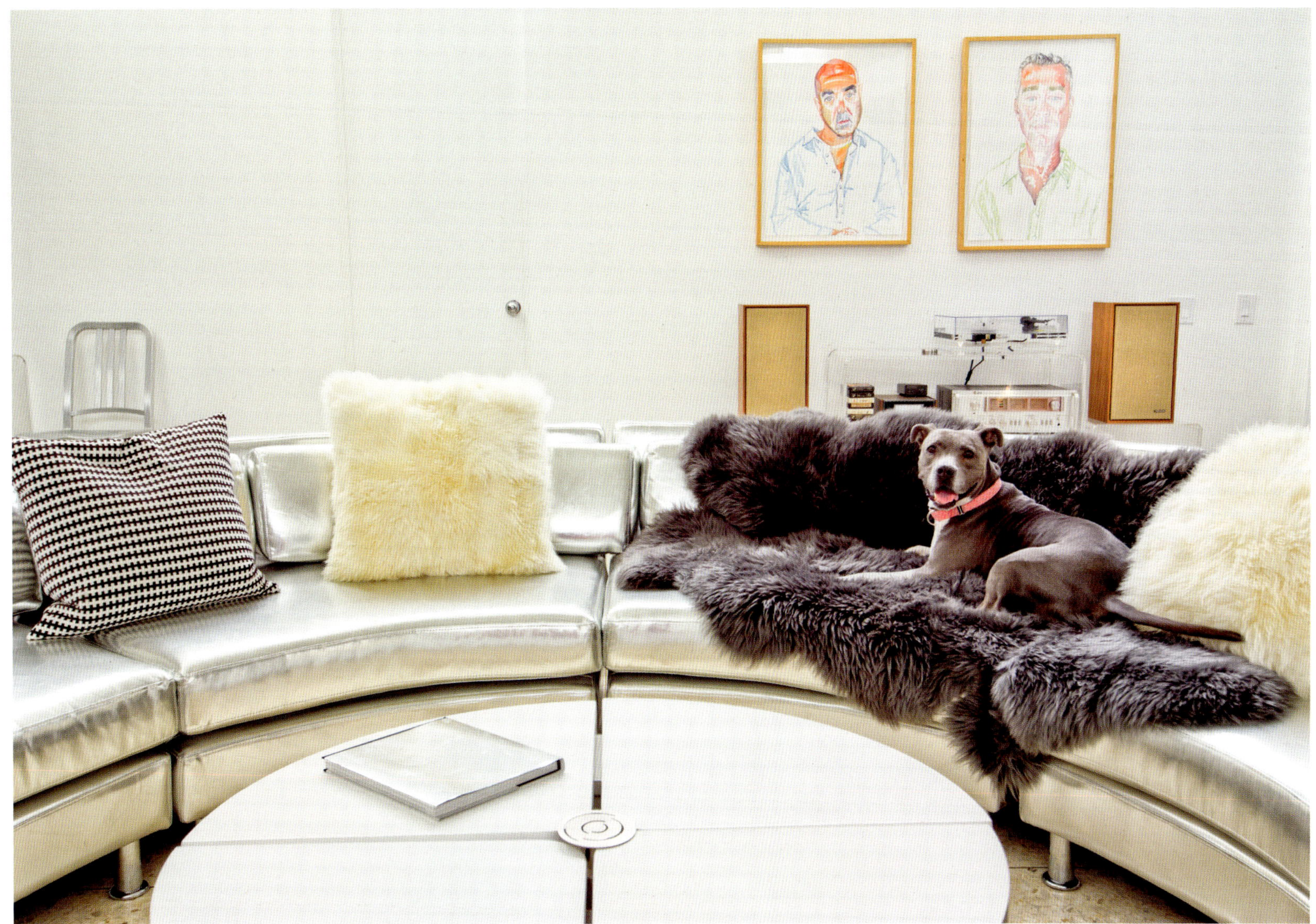

Rocky

JACK RUSSELL TERRIER

ARCHITECT: RICHARD HARRISON, 1966

Rocky is such an integral part of my midcentury modern lifestyle. Just seeing her relaxed, content, and lying in the sun makes me happy.

I love the indoor-outdoor flow of my Palm Springs home; the architectural, stamped concrete; the walls of glass; and the breathtaking views of the mountains from both patios—and the moon is so large at night in the desert sky, it's like you can almost touch it. I feel at one with nature in the desert!

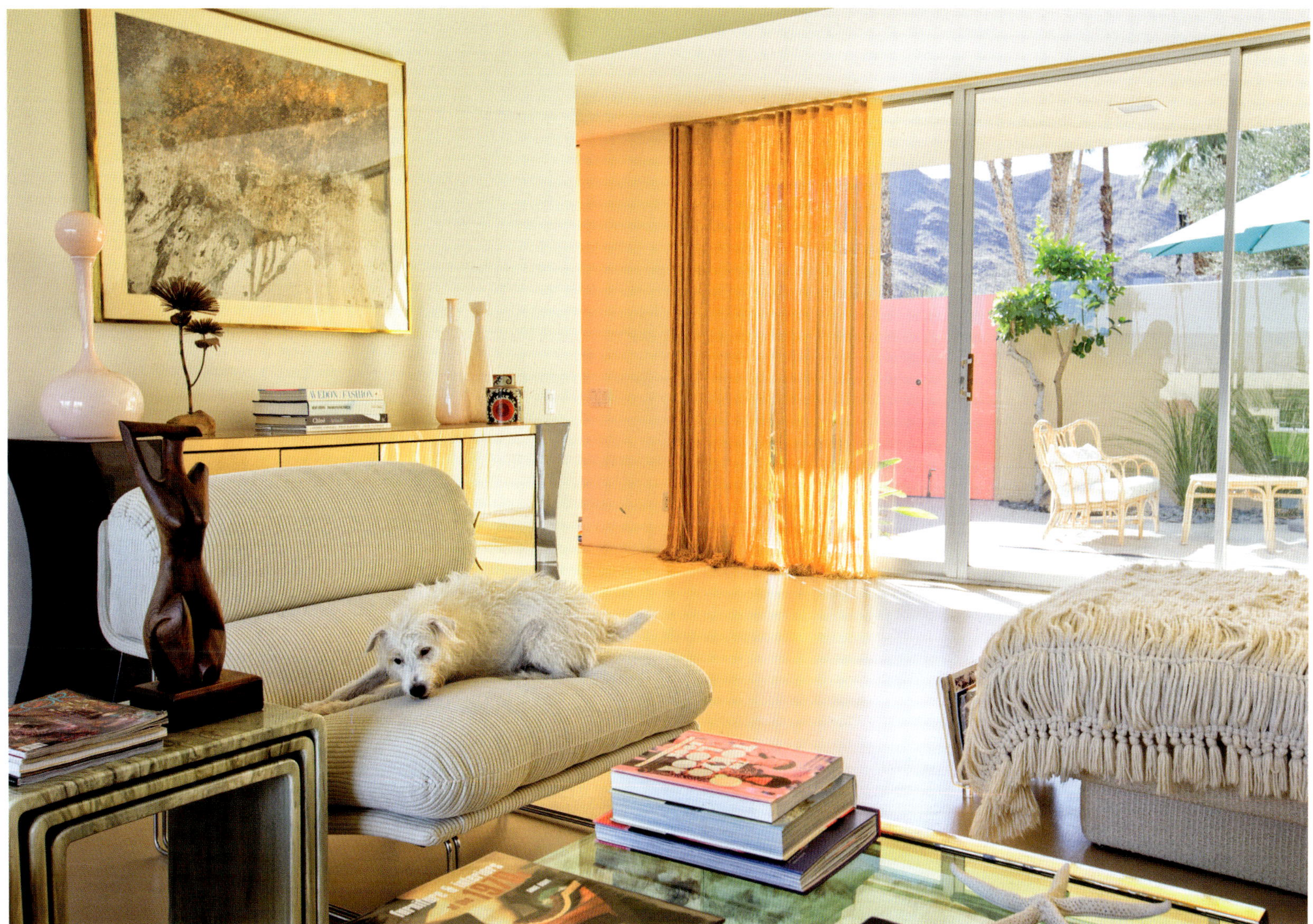

Little Man

**CAVALIER KING CHARLES SPANIEL
RESCUE**

**ARCHITECT: DONALD WEXLER, 1957
THE HOME IS KNOWN AS THE LEFF-FLORSHEIM HOUSE**

Little Man brings an enthusiastic energy to discovering the wonders of living in the desert every day.

Palm Springs and its midcentury modern neighborhoods draw an amazing array of interesting people with a strong appreciation for design, preservation—and dogs!

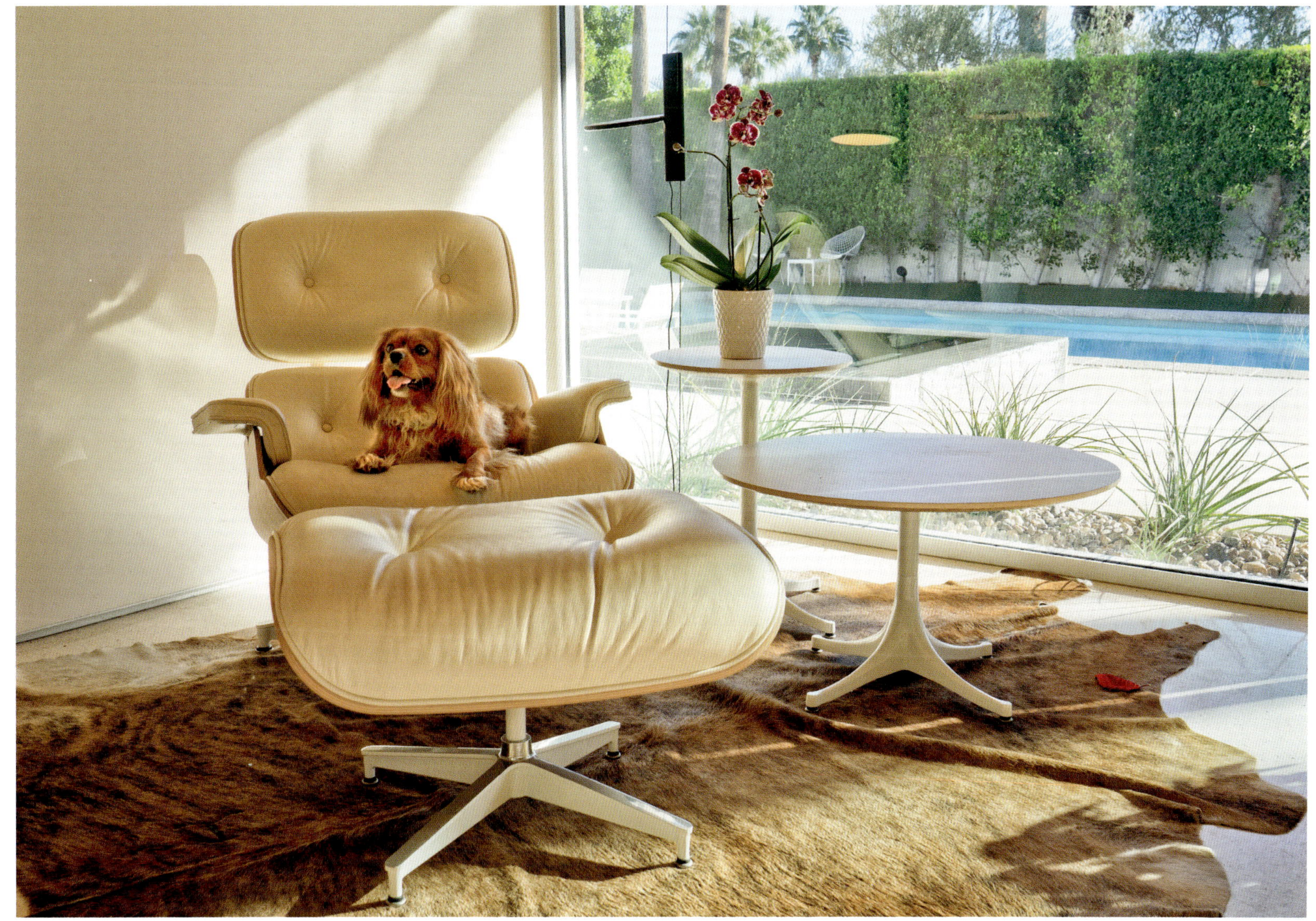

Rhen (L) and Raven

PHU QUOC RIDGEBACKS

ARCHITECT: JACK MEISELMAN, 1958

Our pets are our family and they bring a great deal of joy to our household. Whether we are going for a walk or hanging out in the backyard, our dogs are always with us and provide us with unconditional love. We can't imagine life without them.

Like most residents, we love the beautiful weather and scenery in Palm Springs. Living in a midcentury modern home with expansive windows allows us to take full advantage of the beautiful mountain and garden views. It is truly a joy to live in our bright and sunny MCM home in Palm Springs.

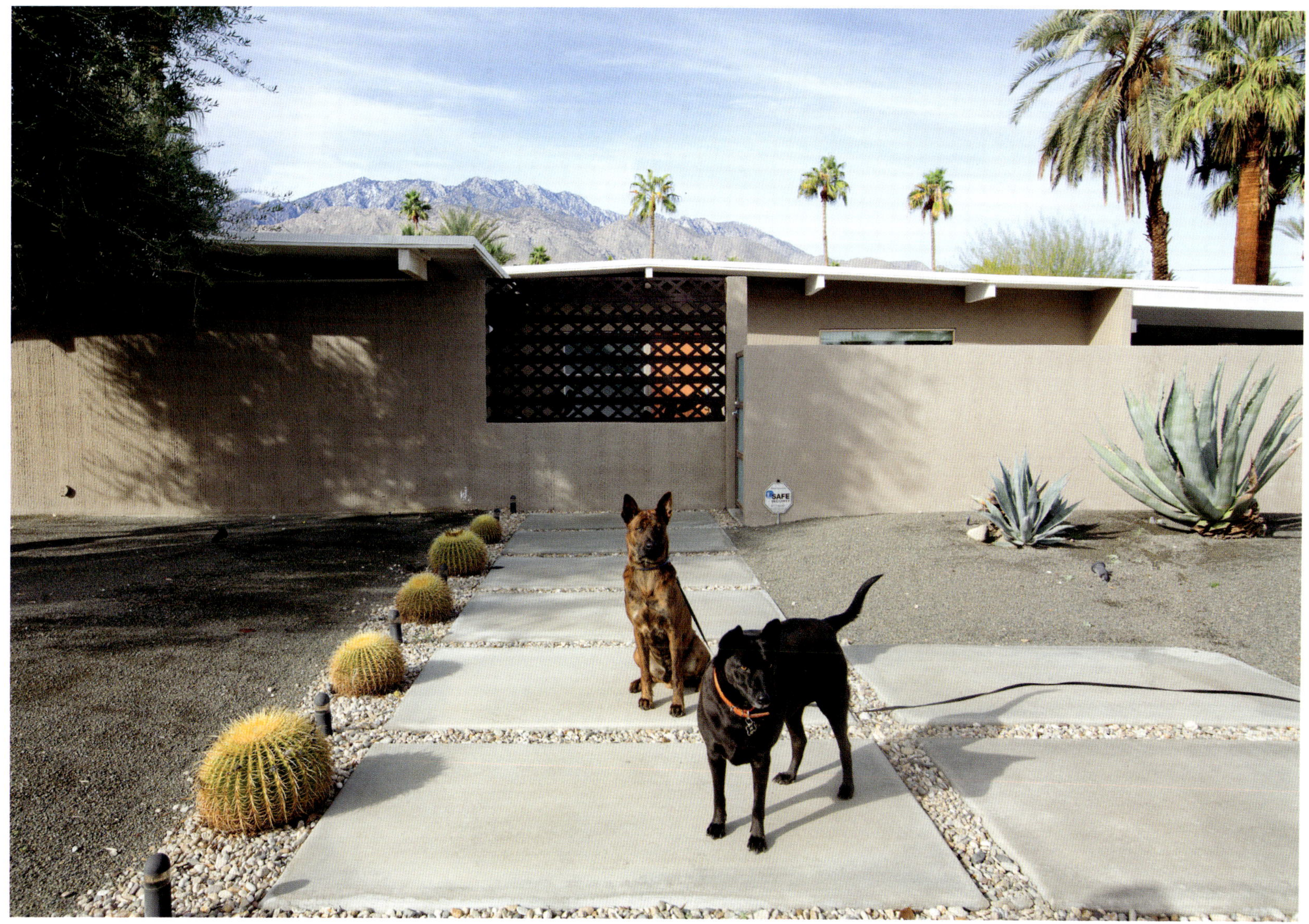

Maddie (Madeleine Simone Dethier)

MIXED BREED
RESCUE

ARCHITECT: JACK MEISELMAN, 1957

I cannot imagine living in a home without pets. Our "dogger" Maddie brings so much warmth and love into our lives and our home, and we are so lucky to be her parents.

The Palm Springs lifestyle is all about easy living, and we enjoy such a high quality of life here in our little desert paradise. Our midcentury modern home is the perfect size—not too big, not too small—and the design allows for full enjoyment of indoor-outdoor living.

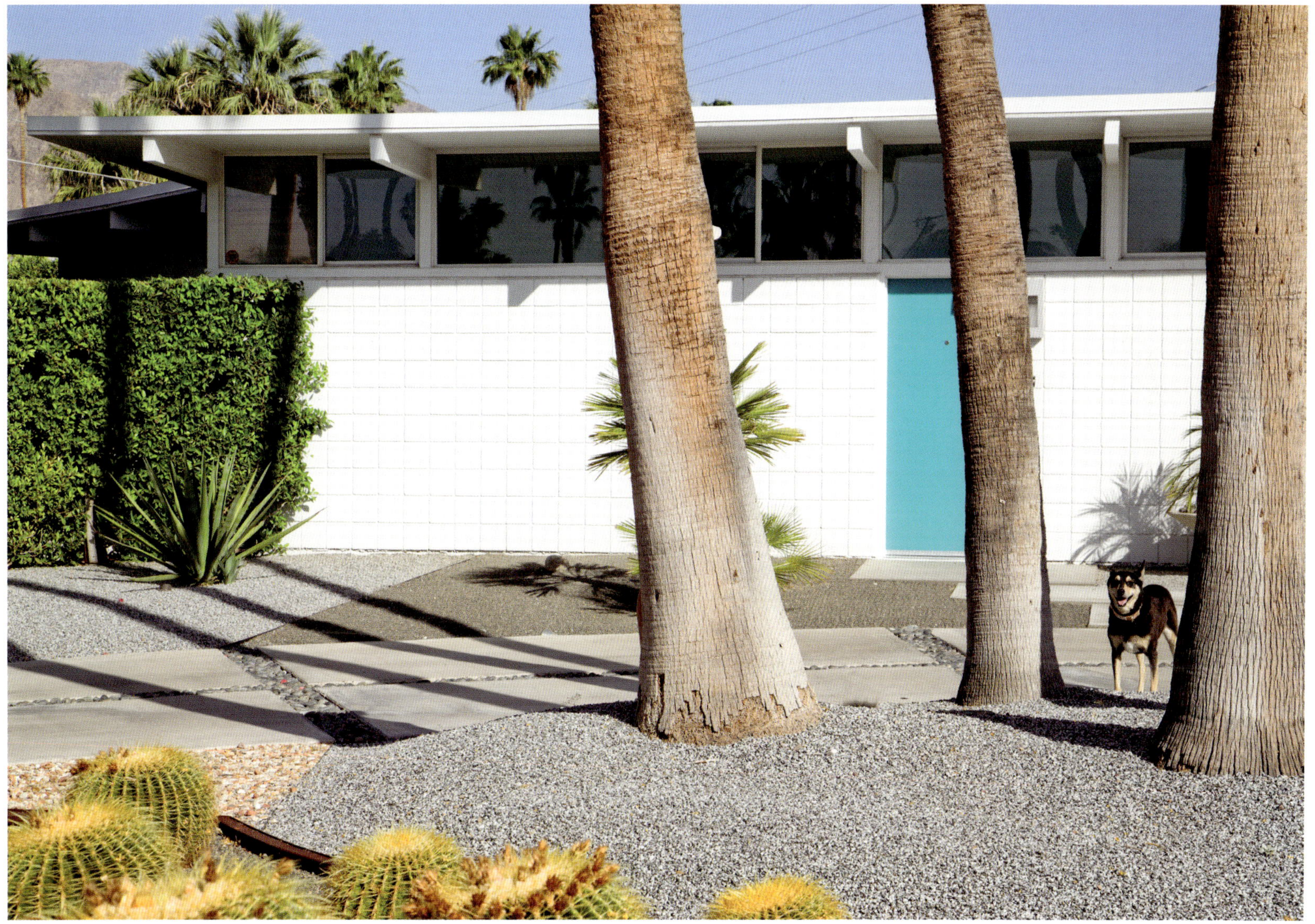

Ozzy

**MIXED BREED
RESCUE**

BUILDER: ALEXANDER CONSTRUCTION COMPANY

The warmth of the sun, clean air, long walks, and rolling around in the grass; this boy enjoys the escape of a weekend in the desert as much as we do.

Midcentury modern design and architecture is the perfect blend of simplicity and sophistication. Time spent in the desert always clears the mind and rejuvenates the soul.

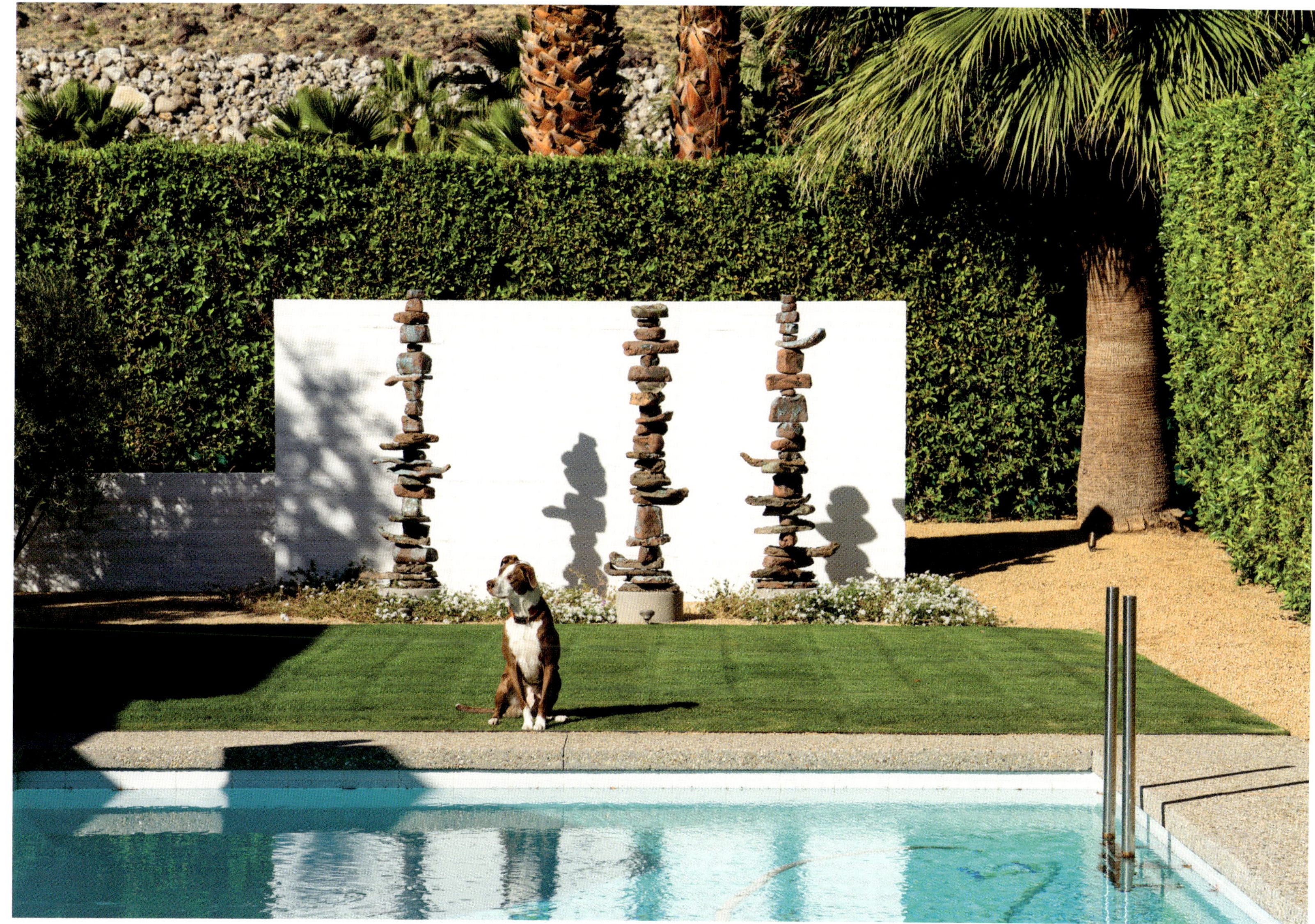

Daisy

**MIXED BREED
RESCUE**

ARCHITECT: WILLIAM KRISEL, 1960

It brings us joy to provide a safe landing for Daisy, who, along with our mixed-breed terrier, Gouda (see p. 50), has faced adversity. It's a pleasure to ensure that her senior years will be secure and comfortable.

We love the '60s era our home represents, with its high ceilings, wood beams, and expanses of glass.

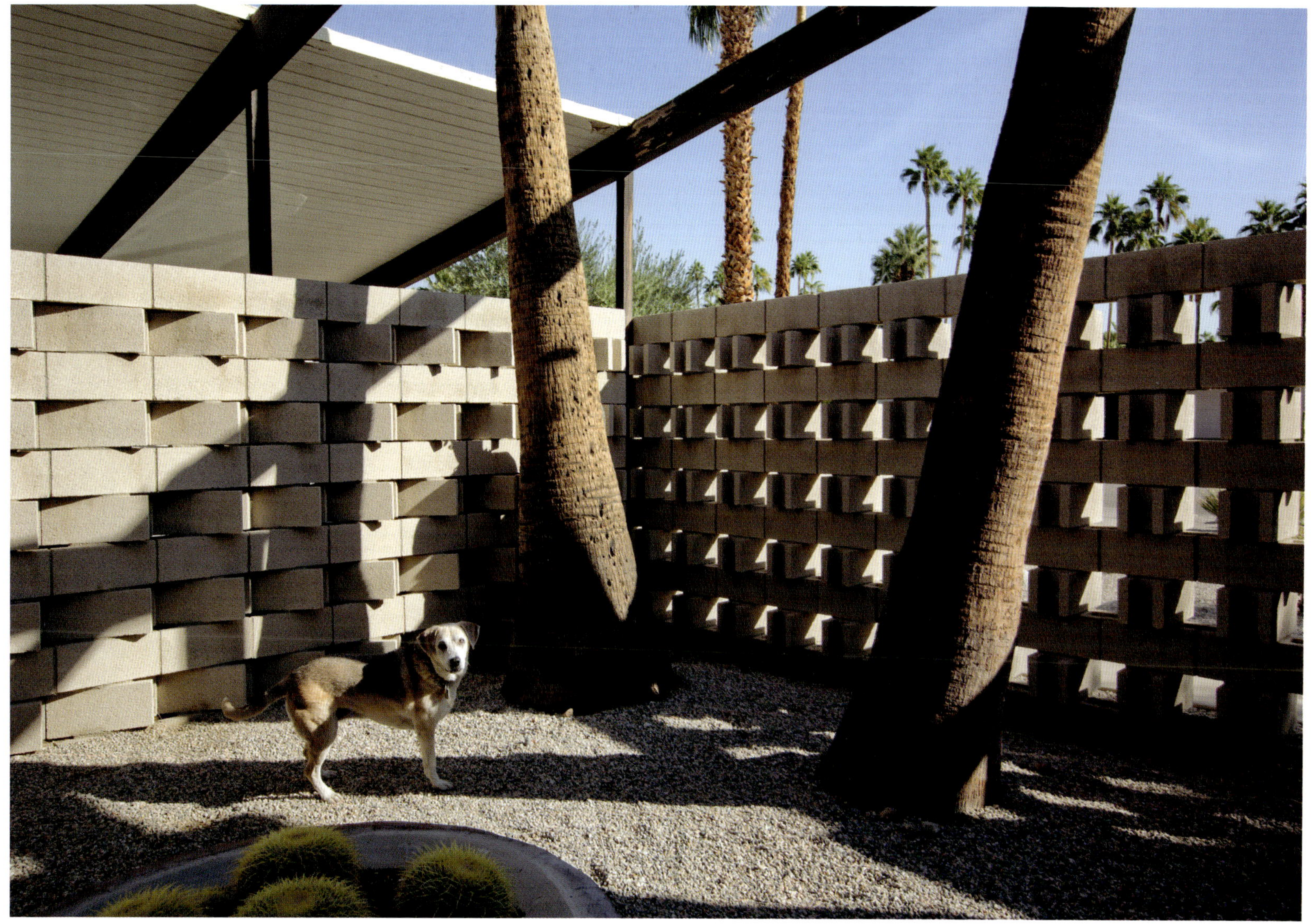

Gouda

TERRIER MIX
RESCUE

ARCHITECT: WILLIAM KRISEL, 1960

Gouda was blind, elderly, and frail when we found him, and the shelter felt he was a "fospice" (foster/hospice) dog because of his poor health, and thought he might live only a few more months. We agreed to bring him home and make him comfortable. That was three years ago. He's thriving.

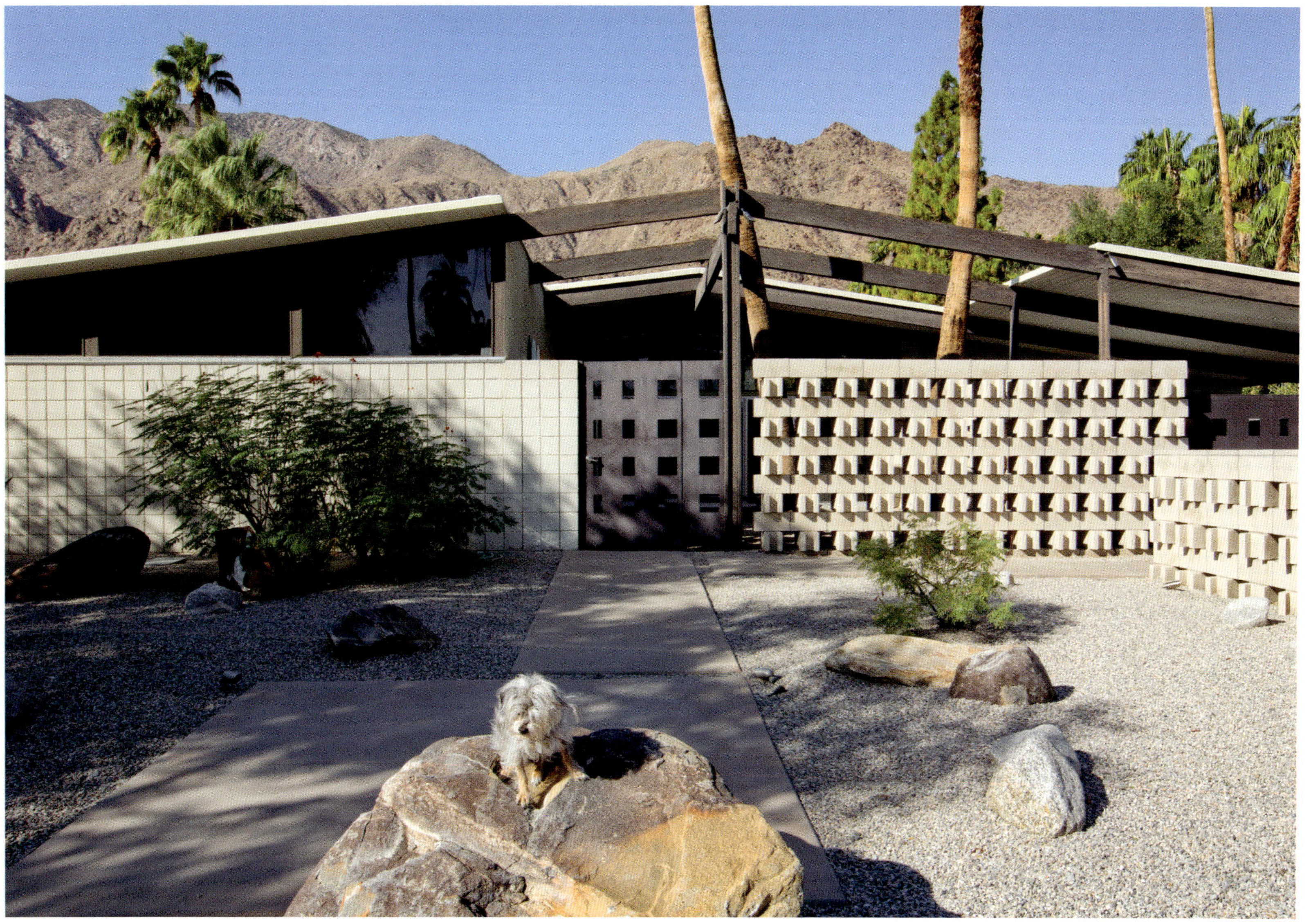

Tippi

BOXER / BULLDOG MIX

ARCHITECT: WILLIAM KRISEL, 1956

Tippi is a lovable, affectionate dog who always enjoys being around people. Her positive energy is contagious, making me smile each and every day.

I don't own an MCM. I'm just an admirer of the aesthetic and overall feeling the homes exude. I am lucky to have friends like Chris who let Tippi and me visit.

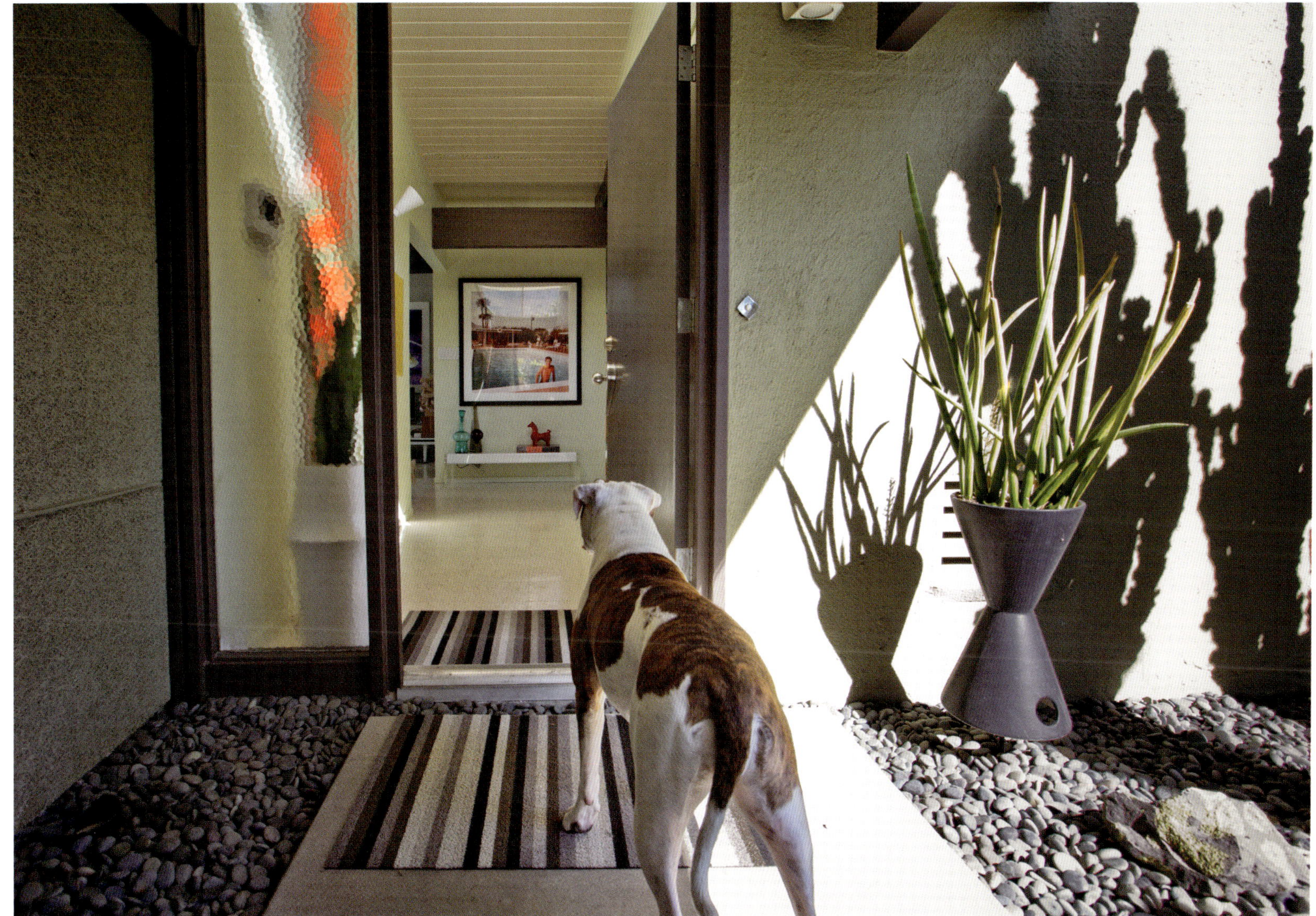

Lou

**RAT TERRIER / CHIHUAHUA MIX
RESCUE**

ARCHITECT: ERIC POON, 2014

Lou's love knows no bounds. We can't imagine life without him. There is nothing better than waking up in the morning and having him crawl out from under the covers and inundate us with hugs and kisses. Can you think of a better way to start the day?

We no longer own a midcentury modern home but own a "this-century modern home."

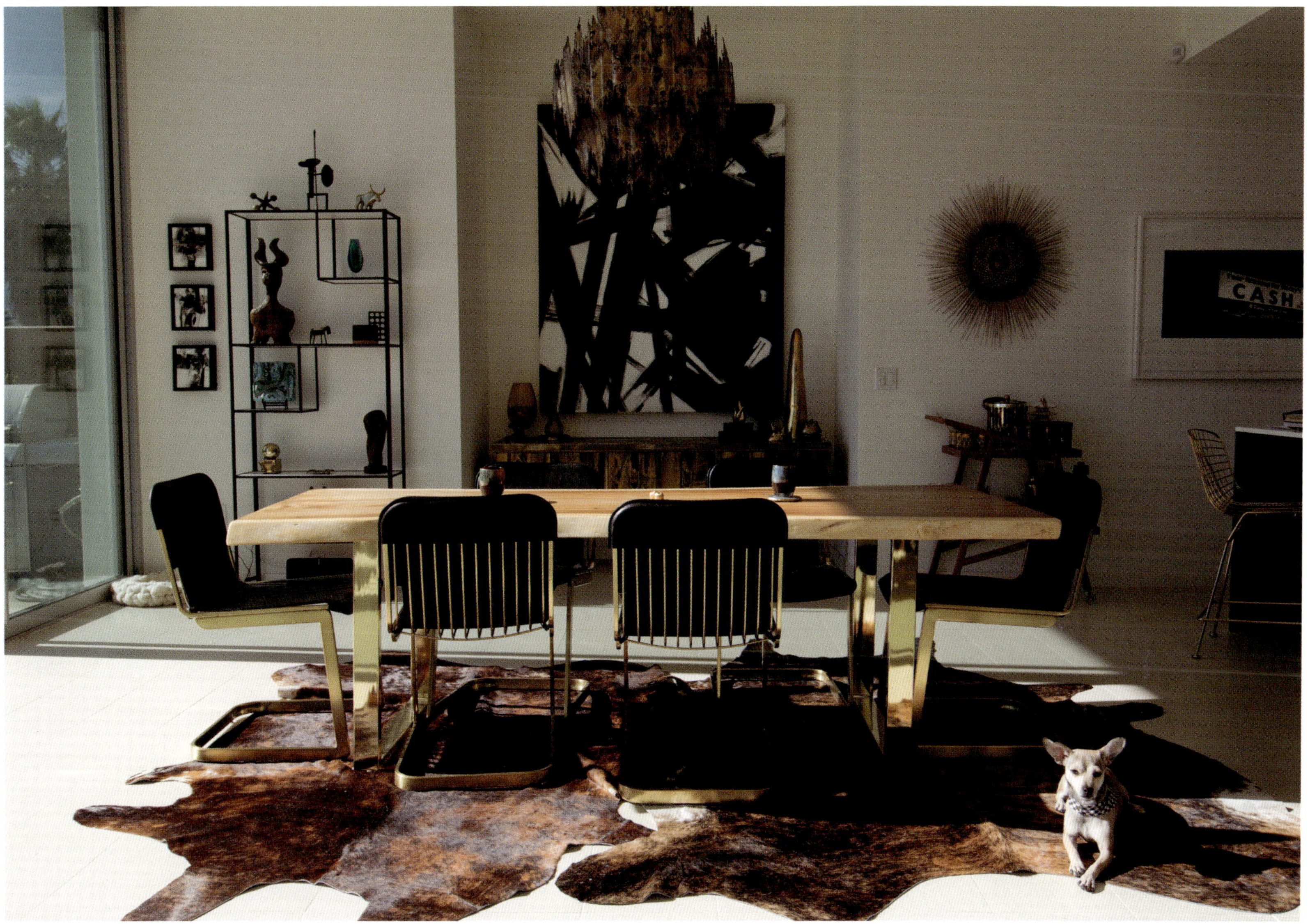

Atticus

**CAIRN TERRIER
RESCUE**

ARCHITECT: HUGH KAPTUR, 1959

After Emerson (see p. 112) died in November 2018, Atticus arrived in late December 2018.

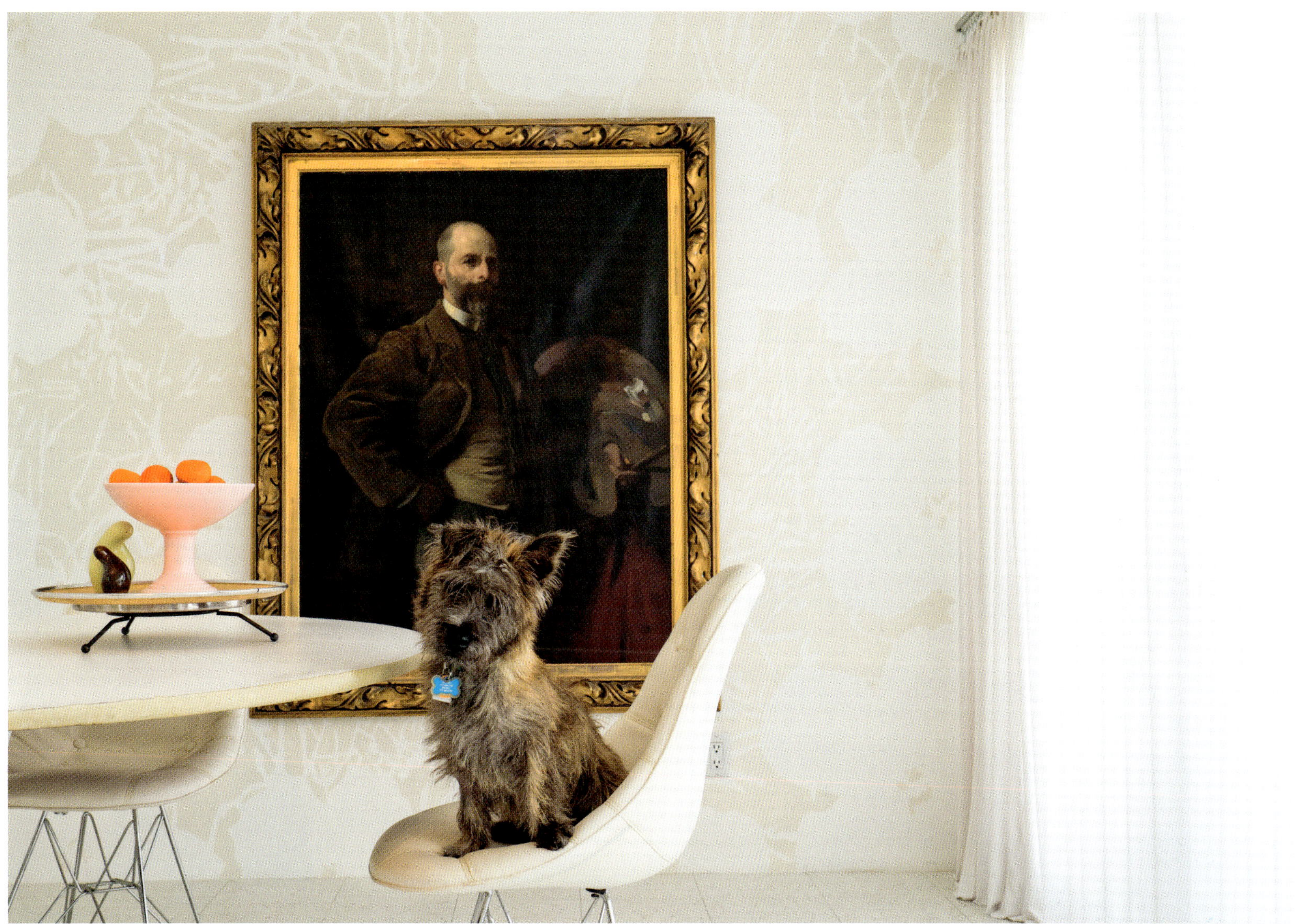

Lenny

**BASSET / PUG MIX
RESCUE**

BUILDER: THE LIBOTT COMPANY, 1957

Lenny moved into this house with us as he had been part of the family for years before. While the grounds are only minimally fenced, he had the privilege of using the enclosed open space between the master bedroom and the garage for personal "needs" between walks. The fact that the house is set high on a hill and near a very steep trail played a part in keeping him fit despite his ravenous appetite. Another aspect of the house that he (and we) enjoyed was an eye-level strip of clear glass that was specifically built into the frosted window so he could keep an eye on the driveway and, accordingly, greet visitors with great enthusiasm.

Our house, despite the fact that it was built over sixty years ago, is still a modern gem with huge volumes of interior space. Its unparalleled view of virtually the entirety of the Coachella Valley provides canines and humans alike the opportunity to survey the landscape in a most panoramic and satisfying way.

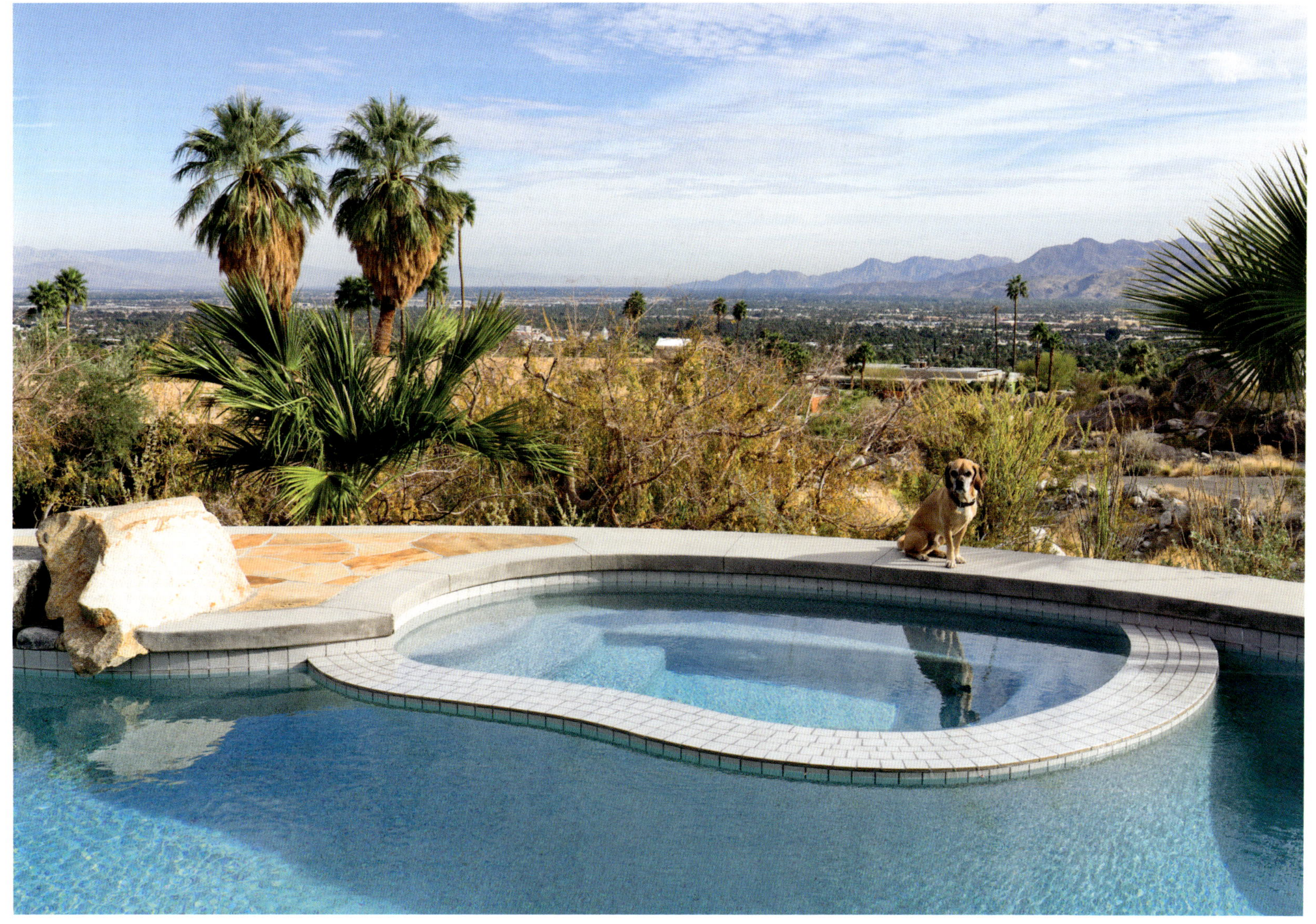

Bunny (L) and Rizzo

**MALTIPOO TERRIER / PINSCHER MIX, CHIHUAHUA MIX
RESCUES**

BUILDER: ALEXANDER CONSTRUCTION COMPANY, 1963

Neither of us had dogs in our adult lives, and it came as quite a shock to discover how much love we could have for two crazy little critters.

We love our home for its simple design, connection to the outdoors, and the spectacular views of the San Jacinto Mountains—without wires!

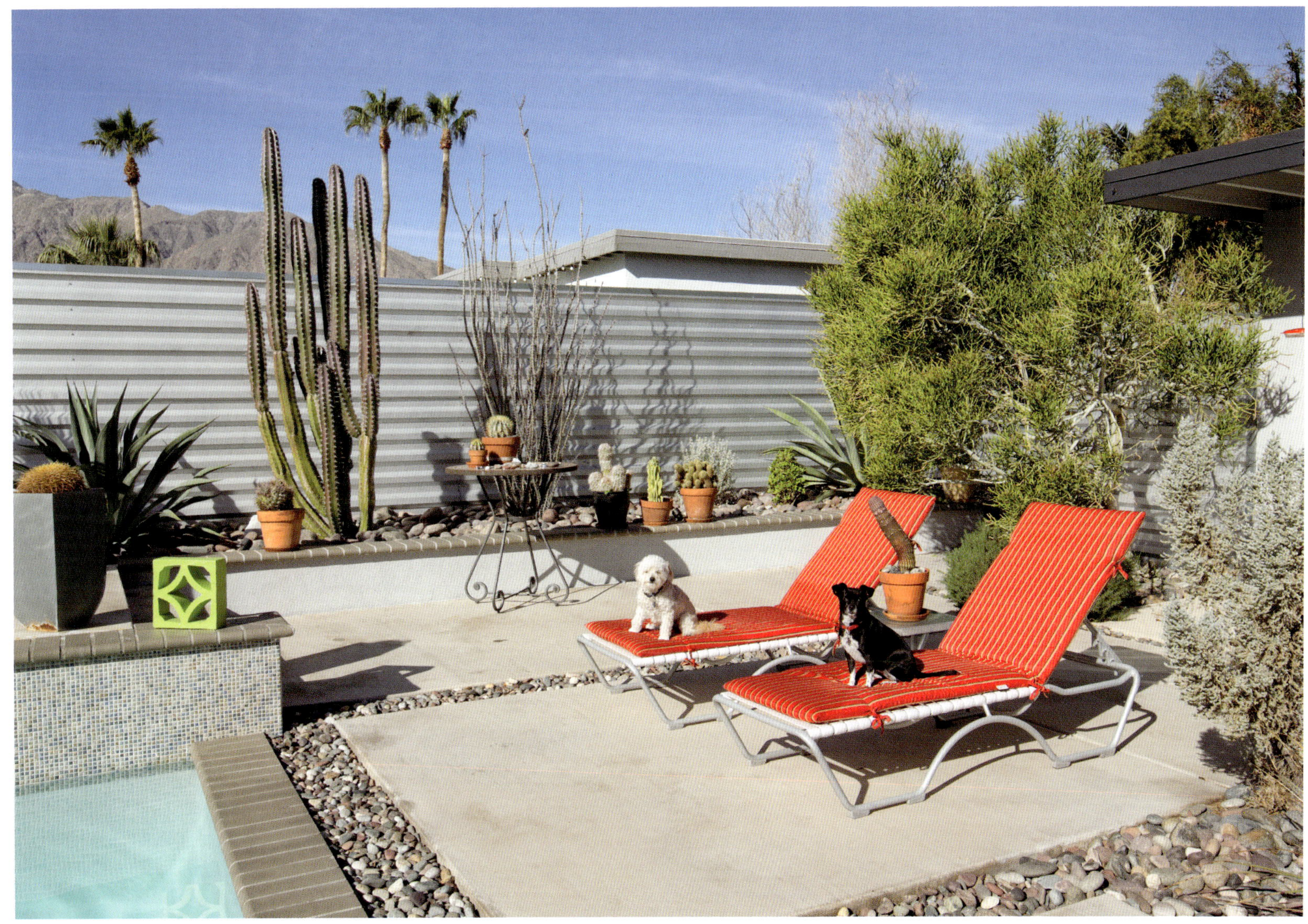

Olive

ENGLISH SHEPHERD

BUILDER: ALEXANDER CONSTRUCTION COMPANY, 1959

Dogs and other animals have always been a part of my home life, so any house without one feels empty and lacking in warmth. Olive has been such a joyful dog—very physically active when she was younger, playing ball and Frisbee until she dropped, and then doing agility courses in class and competition until she was about eight. She's almost fourteen now, but she ran the agility course last week without a hitch. She's amazing!

I love the relaxed pace of Palm Springs, which I feel as soon as I see the wind farms from the 10 freeway. Then, when we arrive at our lovely, cool, sleek MCM house, I know I'm ready for a few days of chilled-out fun.

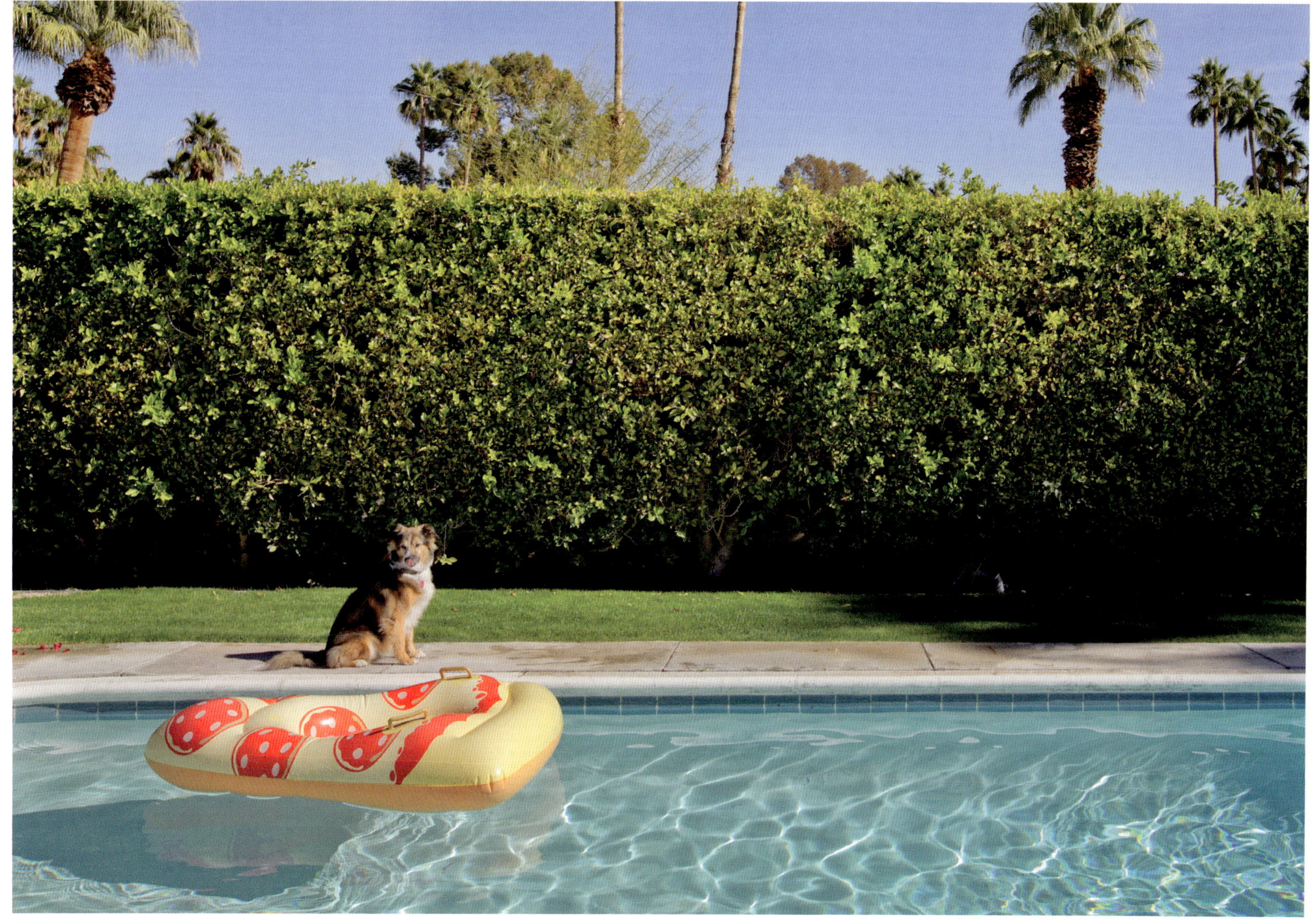

Roxie (L, rescue) and Johnny

JACK RUSSELL / CHIHUAHUA, JACK RUSSELL / DACHSHUND

ARCHITECT: WILLIAM KRISEL, 1964

Without my pups, I would probably sit in front of my computer and work all day. I love going for morning walks and playing fetch in the backyard. They bring so much joy and love into my life.

I love the clerestory windows in my home. They provide the perfect view of the San Jacinto Mountains and the amazing Palm Springs sunsets.

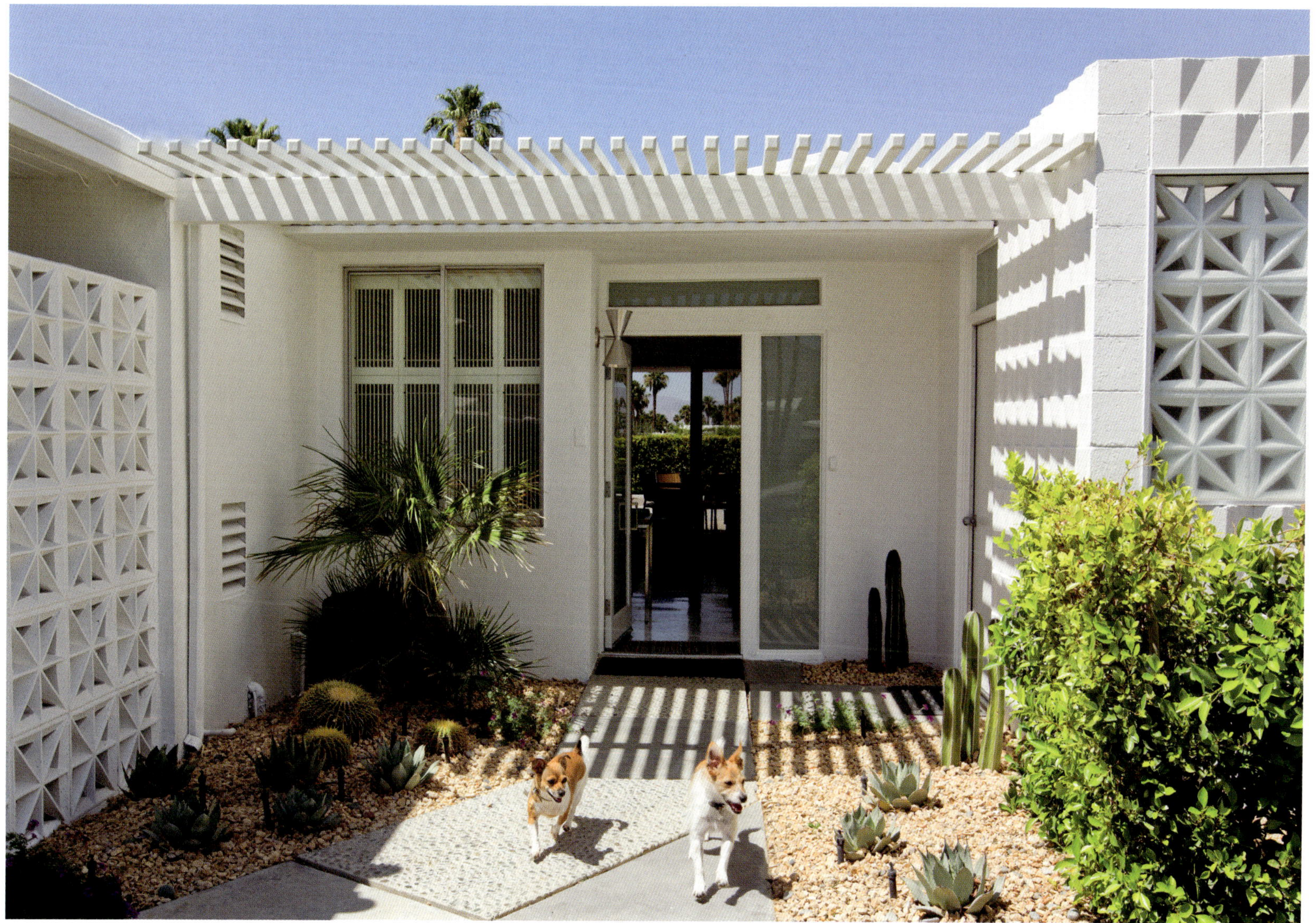

Kirby

**WHEATON / CHOW MIX
RESCUE**

ARCHITECTS: DAN PALMER AND WILLIAM KRISEL, 1964

*I have had rescue dogs since 1980. My home offers natural light and mountain views.
The large patio gives Kirby outdoor space to patrol and to sunbathe. He loves the sun!*

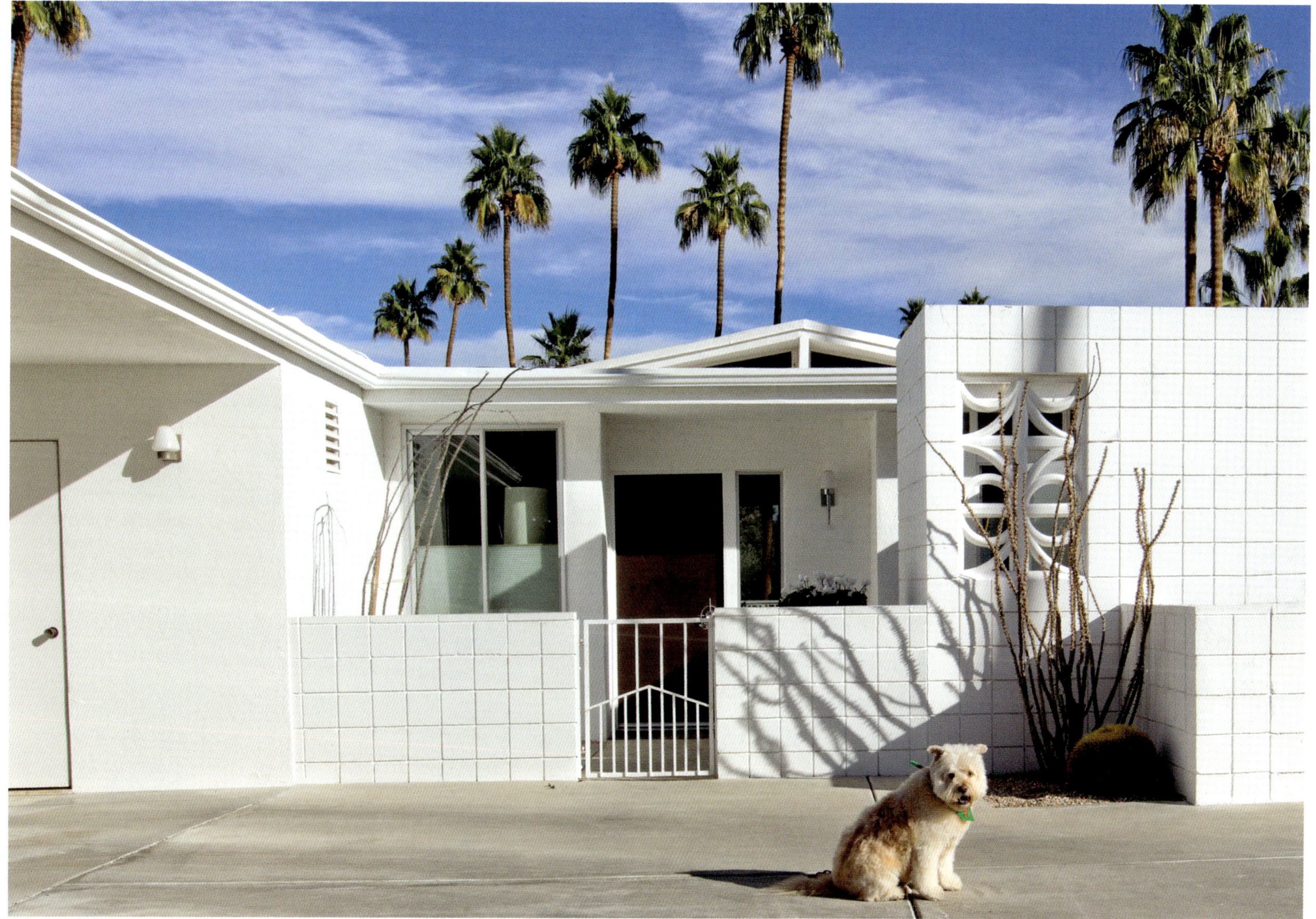

Ruby (L) and Pearl

MAL-SHI, TEDDYBEAR

ARCHITECT: WILLIAM J. O'BRIEN, JR., 1957

We like to tell people that we are very rich because we have a Ruby (left) and a Pearl!

Palm Springs has a wonderful architectural heritage and history. Living in a midcentury modern home makes us feel like we're a part of that.

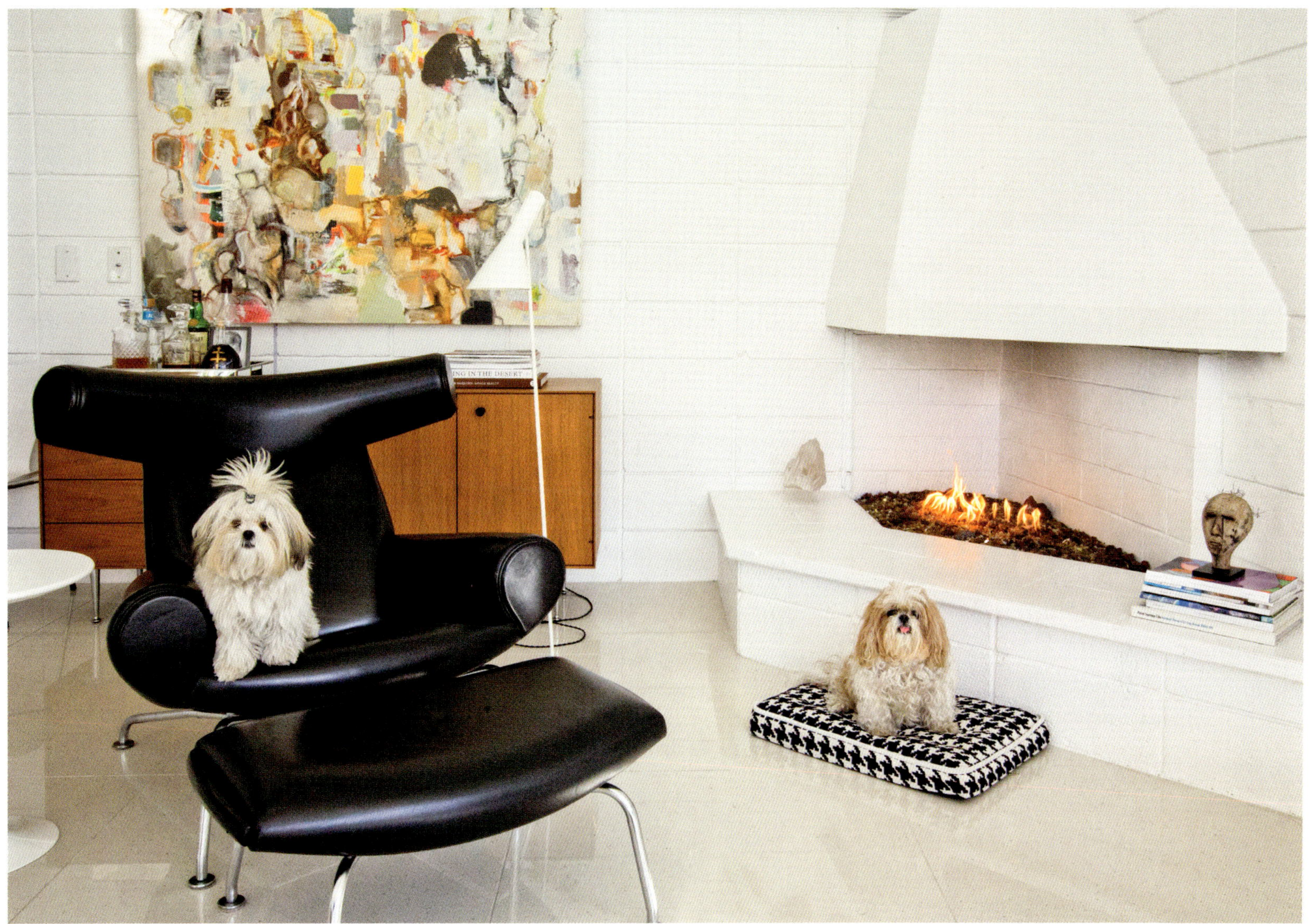

Sidney (L) and Olivia

**MIXED BREED
RESCUES**

CANYON COUNTRY CLUB TRACT DEVELOPED BY HARRY KELSO, 1964

For us, a house doesn't feel like a home without our dogs. They bring joy wherever they go.

We love the brilliant desert light and the imposing mountains of Palm Springs. Midcentury architecture, with its expanses of glass and clean lines, is both the perfect complement and striking contrast to the desert landscape. Can't get enough!

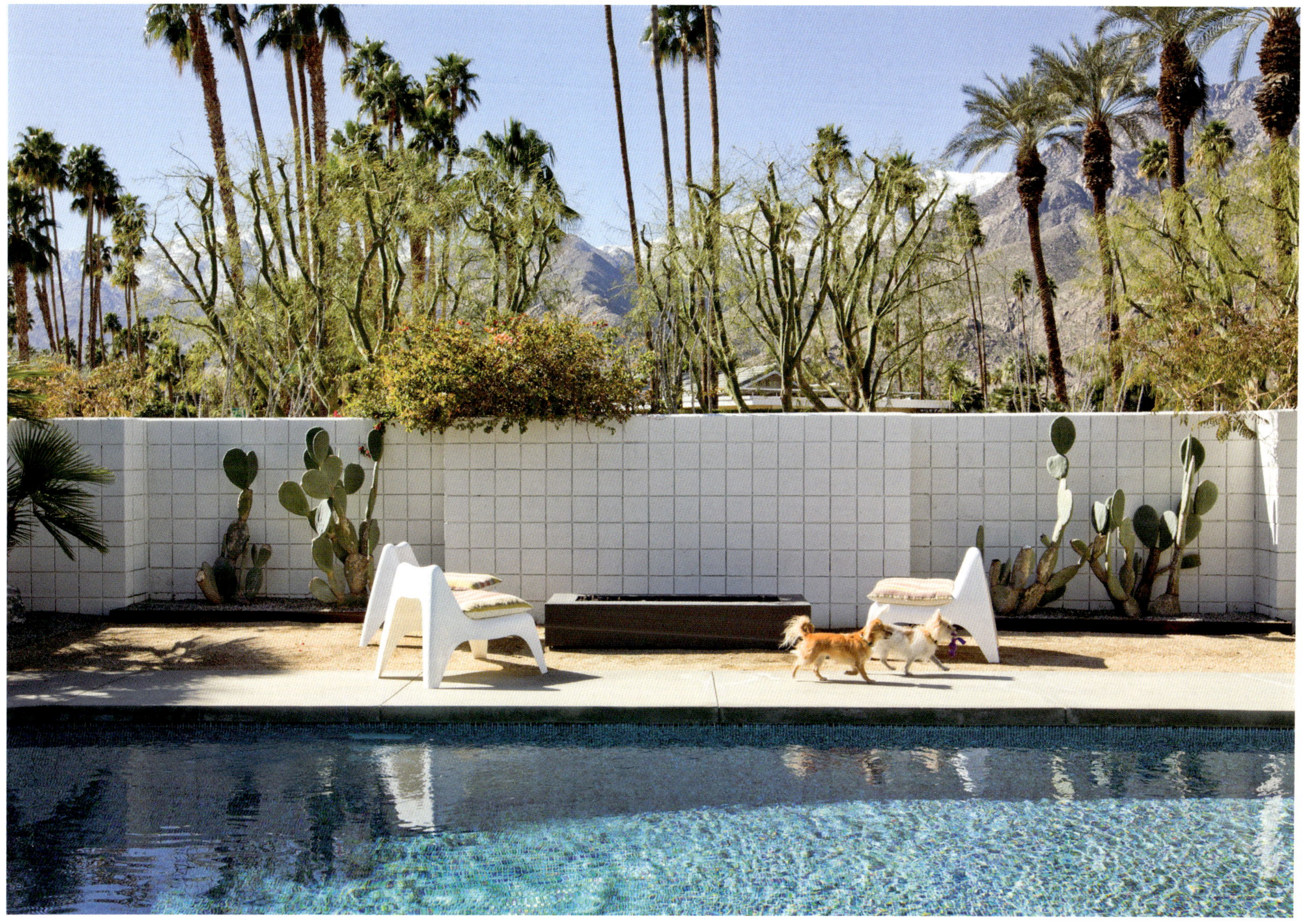

Gizmo

MIXED BREED
RESCUE

ARCHITECTS: BARRY BERKUS AND WILLIAM BONE, 1972

I moved to Palm Springs full time five years ago with Gizmo for a fresh start. Our home is cozy and comfortable and fits with our lifestyle—enjoying all the activity here in Palm Springs. There's so much to do! Gizmo and I are regulars downtown at several of the pet-friendly eateries. We've made lots of new friends here in Palm Springs, done some volunteer work, and had lots of fun! Of course, it wouldn't be possible without my little buddy, "The Giz."

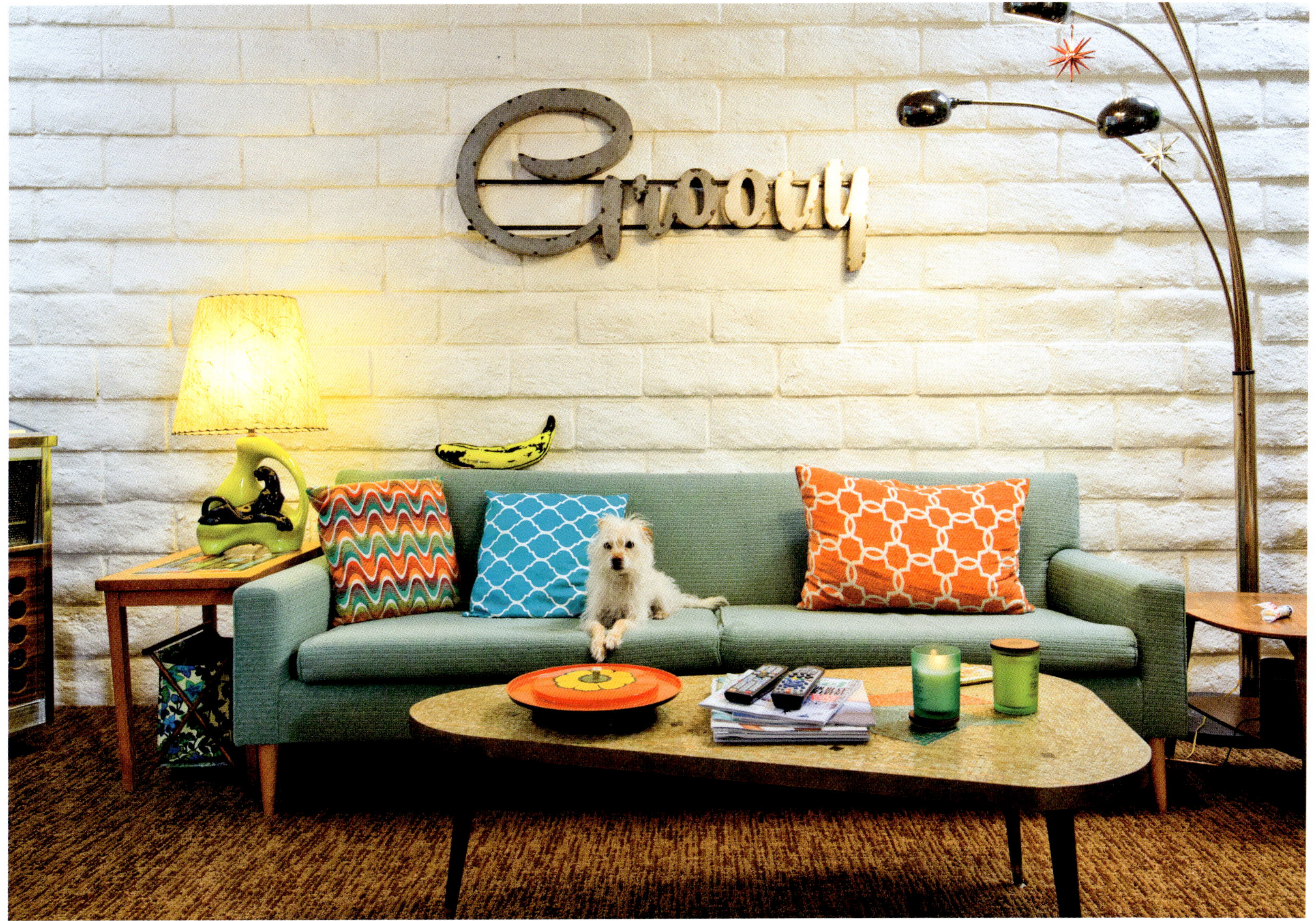
Groovy

Rocky

**AKITA (AMERICAN)
RESCUE**

BUILDER: SAM PASCAL, 1956

Dogs bring an abundance of joy and love to our home!

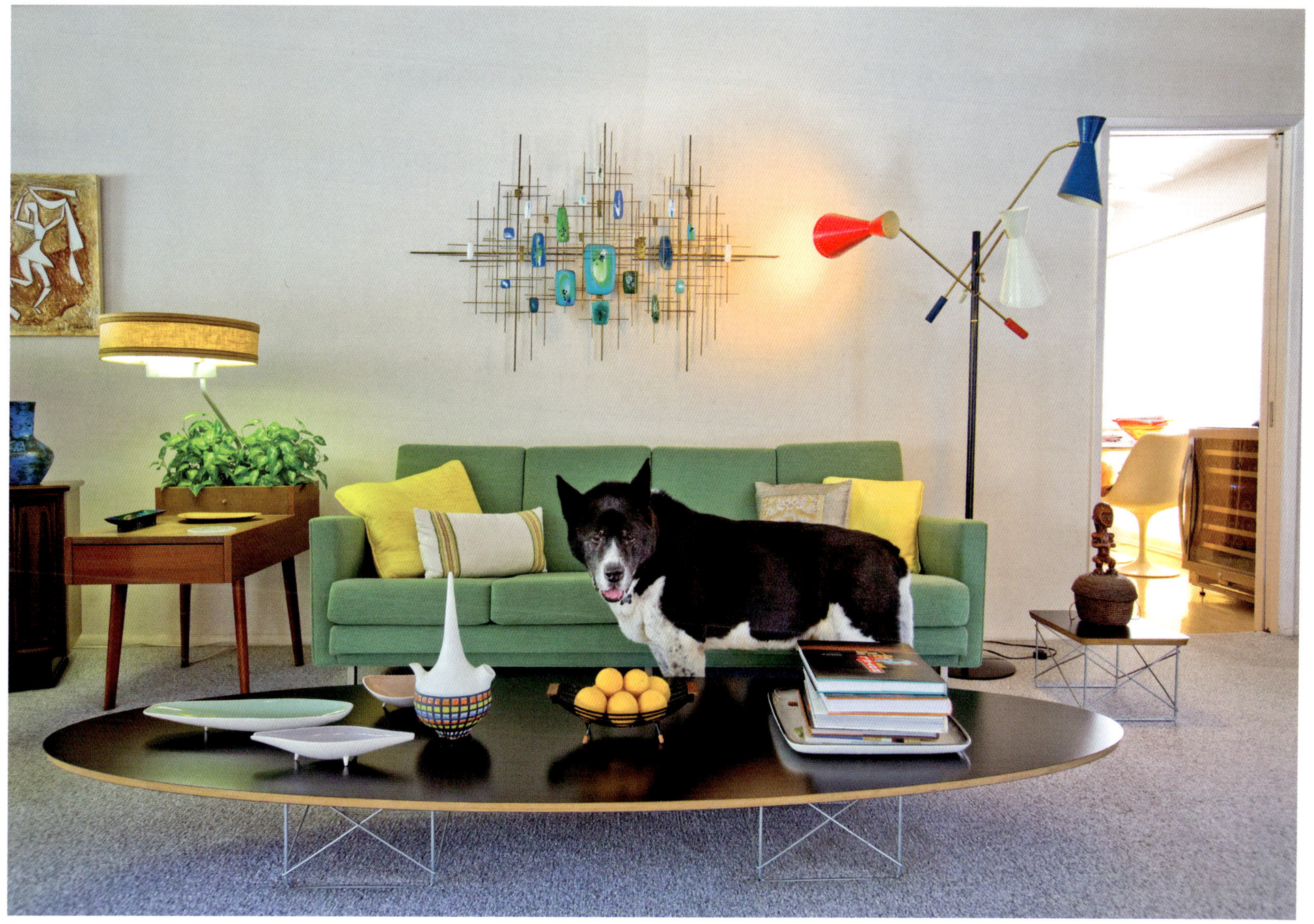

Busy

**MINI FOX TERRIER MIX
RESCUE**

**ARCHITECT: ROBERT MEYERS AND VICTOR KOOZI, 1966
CAR: 1975 DELTA 88 ROYALE CONVERTIBLE**

Busy is adorable all day long. He's a bundle of energy and all smiles and sunshine. He loves a sunbath and especially enjoys all the classic car and trailer shows he gets to attend.

MCM is appealing because of the simplicity in design, and I like the many variations and styles within MCM.

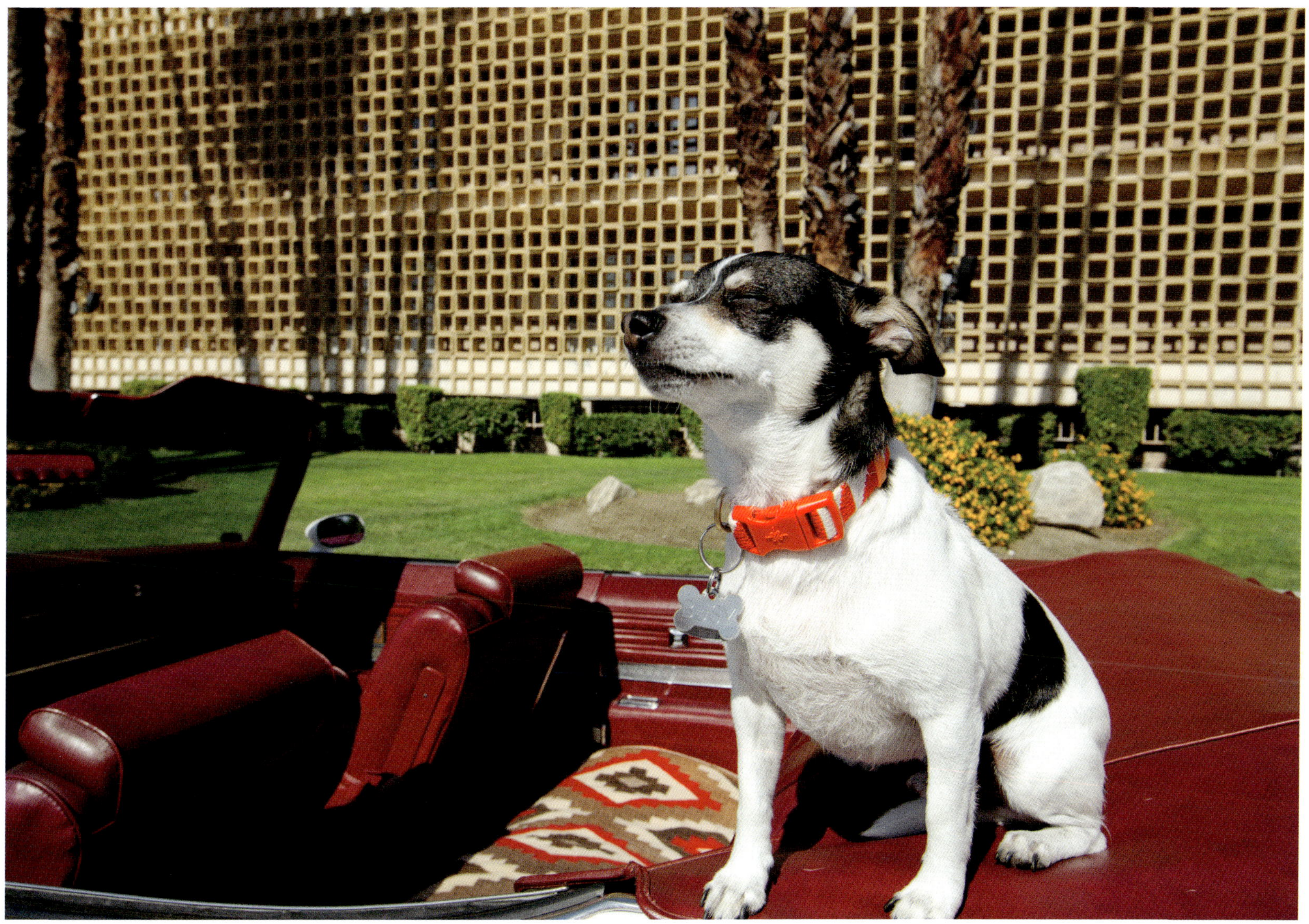

Blanca

**RAT TERRIER / CHIHUAHUA MIX
RESCUE**

ARCHITECT: HERBERT BURNS, 1950

We've had other dogs in the past, but Blanca has such a personality, is so intelligent, and really communicates what she is thinking and feeling (and what she wants you to do for her, NOW!). I can't imagine life without her now that we've had her for four years.

We moved to Palm Springs because we found this house. We have long collected furniture designed by Gilbert Rohde for Herman Miller, a collection from 1941. Most modern houses in Palm Springs feature post-and-beam construction, and while we appreciate that, Herbert Burns designed in the same late moderne style as our Rohde furniture. There are so few houses by Burns; we had to have it!

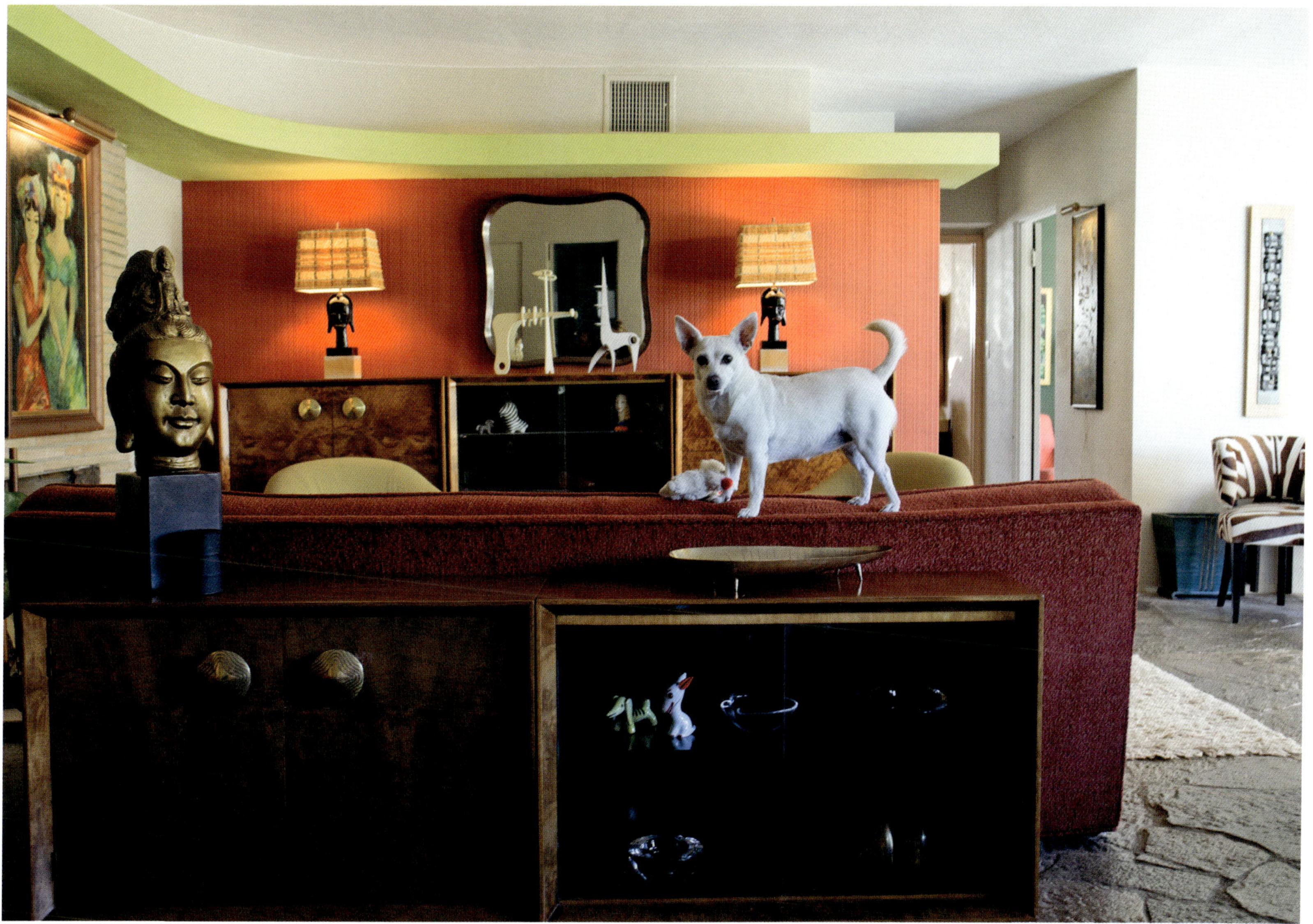

Tony

AIREDALE

FEY DEVELOPMENT, 1978

Our high-spirited and mischievous Airedale is a great representative of his breed. His structure and elegance are architectural, as befits Palm Springs. Tony is a great companion to one of us who has PTSD from serving in the Marine Corps.

We are designers. Midcentury architecture and design are a part of our overall lifestyle. We consider Palm Springs to be a world-class city, attracting creative residents involved in the arts and architecture.

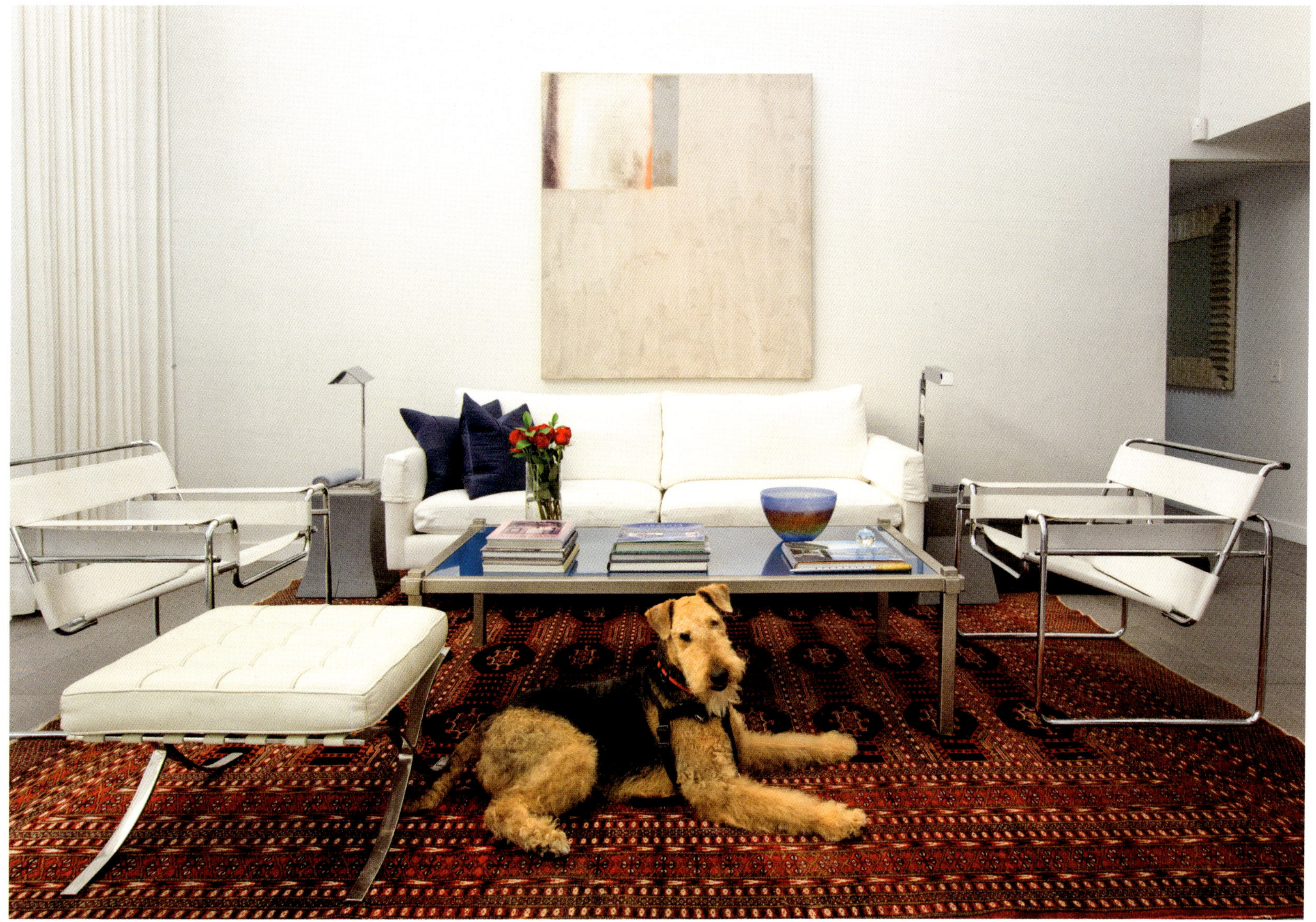

Joey

MINIATURE DACHSHUND

ARCHITECT: DONALD WEXLER, 1959

Even though Joey is "sweet sixteen," he still acts like a puppy. He loves to play, is super cuddly, loves a good hike (just a little slower these days), and warms up easily to new people and other dogs. He also keeps our kitchen floors clean! Ha! Joey loves going to the Palm Springs pad. Just like us, he loves the sun—he even lounges in the pool on a raft.

When we updated our home, we wanted to keep the midcentury vibe but add an earthy, updated feel. It's modern, but inviting and warm. Our small community and neighbors at El Rancho Vista Estates are fantastic. Everyone has a deep appreciation for midcentury modern design and are very down to earth and fun to be around. As soon as we hit the door in our Wexler home, we instantly relax. There is something about Palm Springs that exudes relaxation. We love the weather, amazing mountain views, wonderful modernism community, and great restaurants.

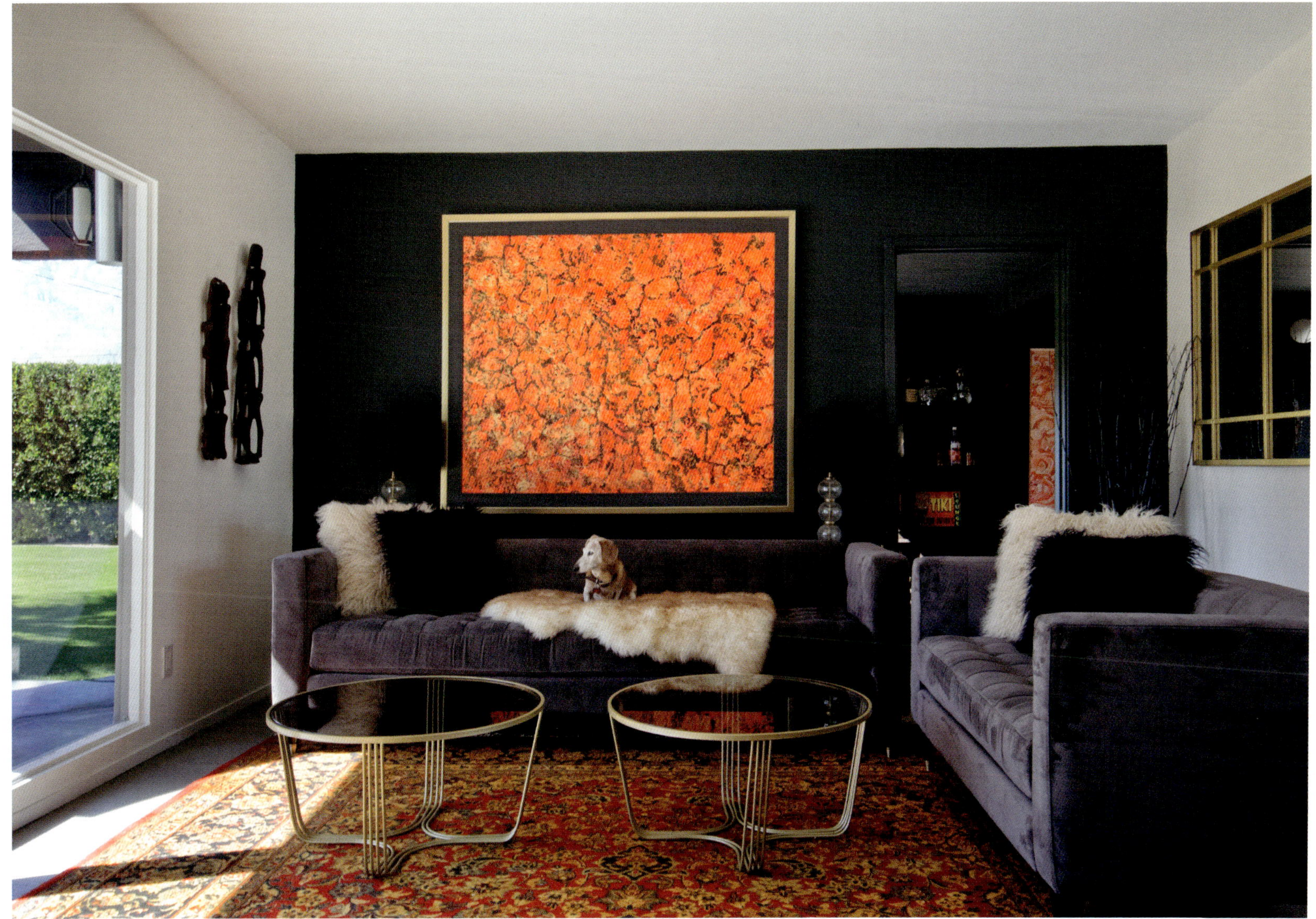

Elio

**JACK RUSSELL / RAT TERRIER / CHIHUAHUA MIX
RESCUE**

ARCHITECT: CHARLES DUBOIS, 1971

We rescued Elio two and a half years ago when he was five months old. Our hearts had been shattered by the sudden loss of our five-year-old, Frenchie. We could not stand to be in our home; it was so lonely without our baby. Elio was an angel from the moment we brought him home. He is a very special, wise, intuitive, and super-loving dog. The spot on the center of his head does allude to spiritual powers in some cultures, and we are true believers!!! We have traveled with him extensively, and he is almost always with us. He makes our house feel like a home—full of love and joy.

Our home is full of light and perfectly reflects the beauty of a sunny Palm Springs day. We have carefully curated our collection of MCM objects, furnishings, art, and lighting from America, Brazil, and Europe—particularly Italy. The high ceilings and many clerestory windows transform our living space into a gallery-like setting. Palm Springs is a magical town full of a very special cast of characters—creative, passionate, and unique people drawn to the beauty of the desert. We feel alive in this environment and around these people!!!

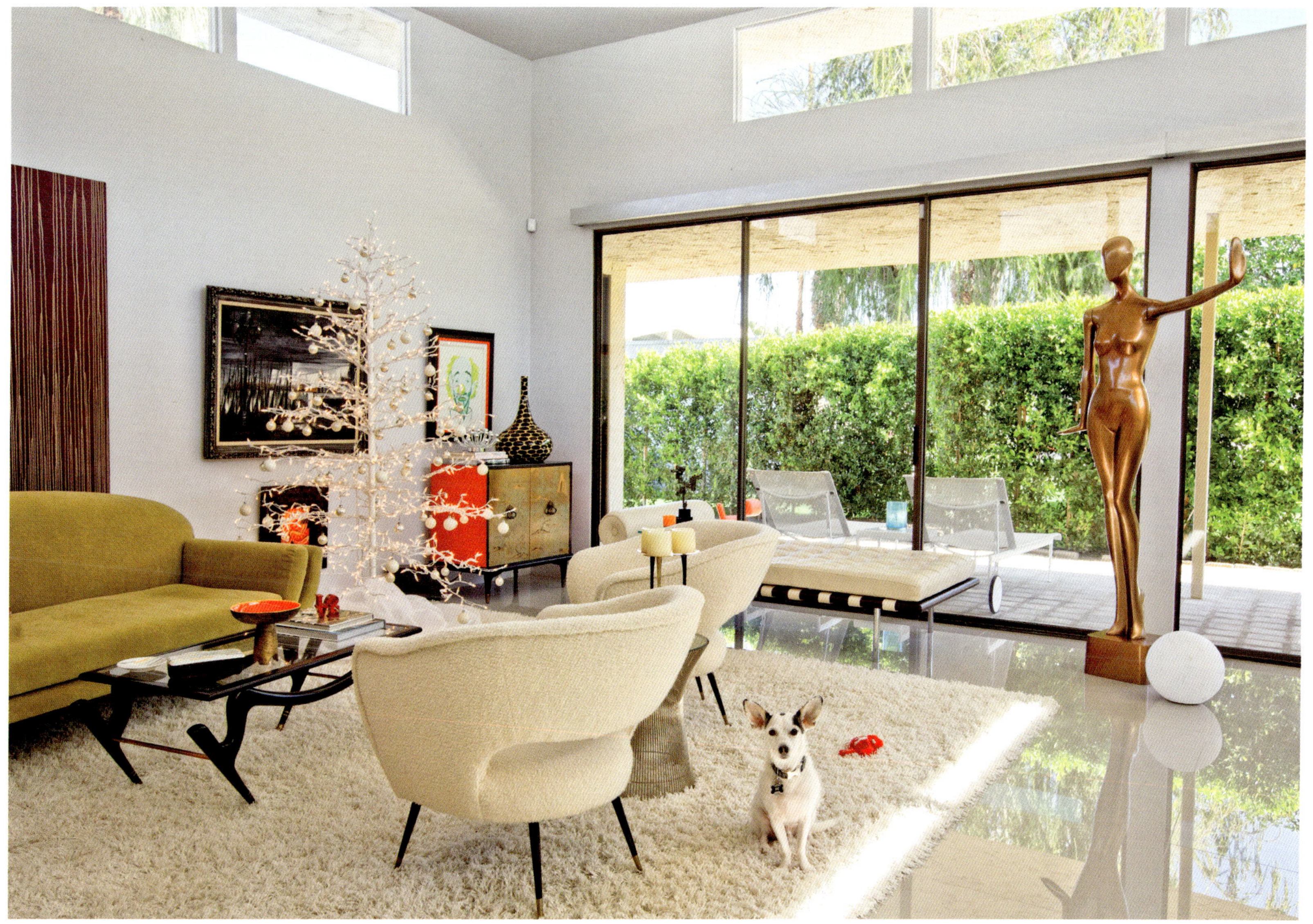

Archie (Archibald Alouicious Chambers)

**BICHON FRISE / TOY POODLE MIX
RESCUE**

ARCHITECT: WILLIAM KRISEL, 1964

*Archie is one of those pets that can't wait to show his affection for any other person
or dog that is friendly toward him. We always say he generates love in the world, and
every day there's a little more love because of him.*

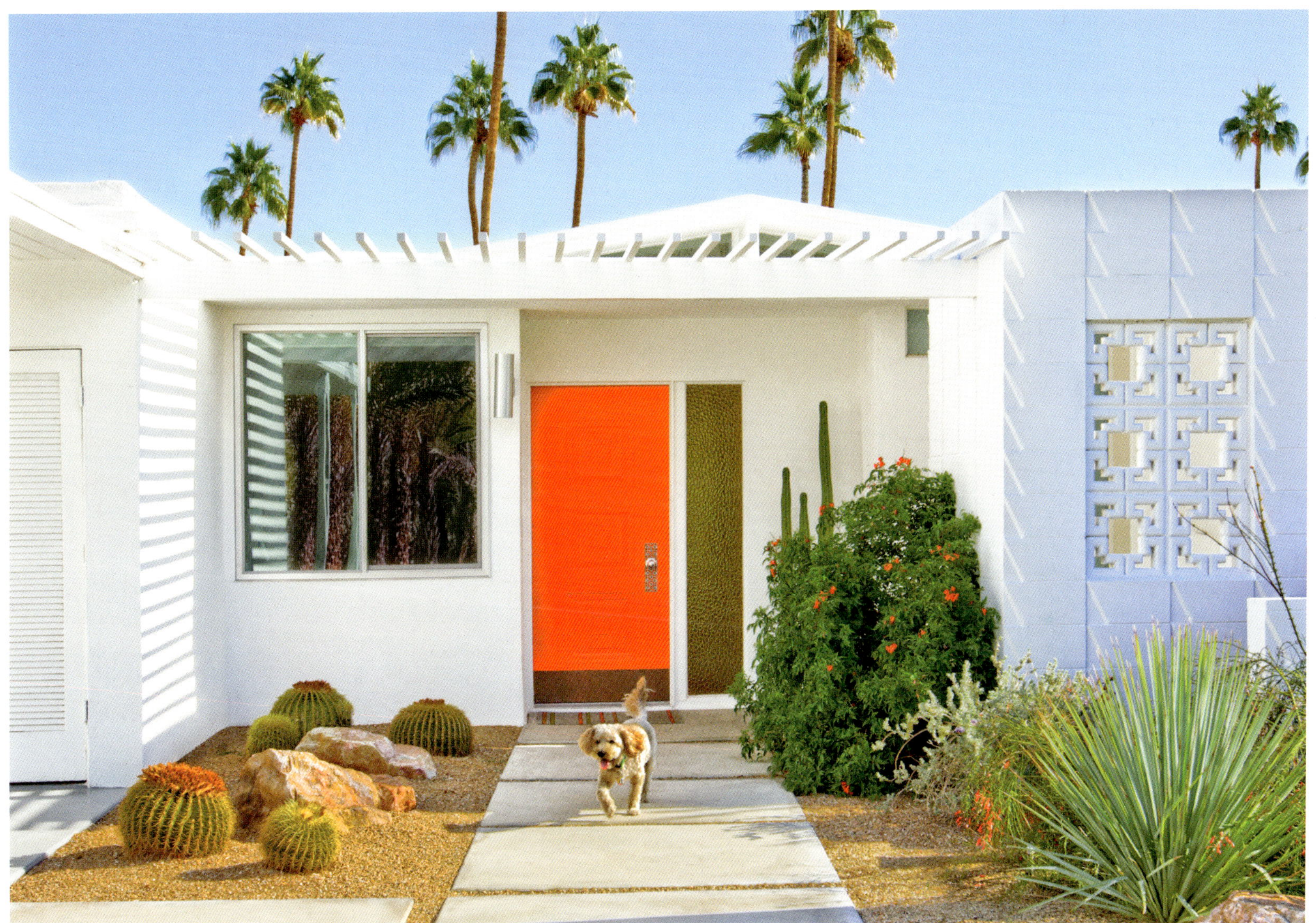

Toffee Nelson-Lowery

JACKAHUAHUA, OR, AS WE LIKE TO SAY, JACKIE-O RUSSELL RESCUE

ARCHITECT: CHARLES DUBOIS, 1962

Toffee is a great guardian of our space and is always watching out for her daddies. Her kisses are the sweetest and we love seeing the joy she gets from tummy rubs!

Our Charles DuBois home is the epitome of Vista Las Palmas midcentury modern living, and its '60s colors feel timeless.

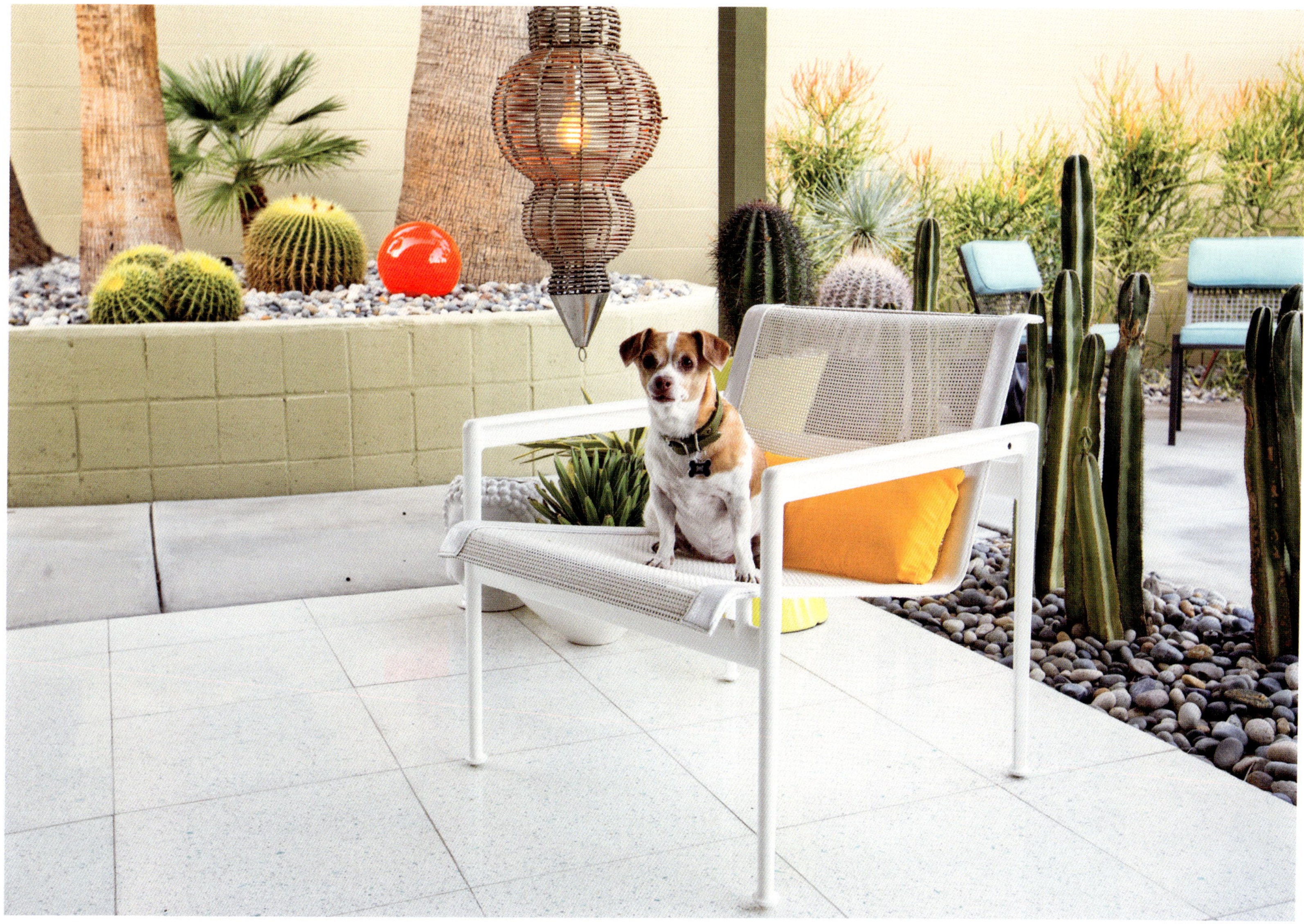

Whiskey Woods

CAVAPOO

BUILDER: ALEXANDER CONSTRUCTION COMPANY, 1959

Whiskey, to us, is the perfect dog—the best combination of lazy and playful. Like a piece of decor, Whiskey is known to lie by the pool for most of the day in true Palm Springs style.

We are at peace in our home; it's comforting, welcoming, and a place where everyone gathers to sip drinks and lie by the pool.

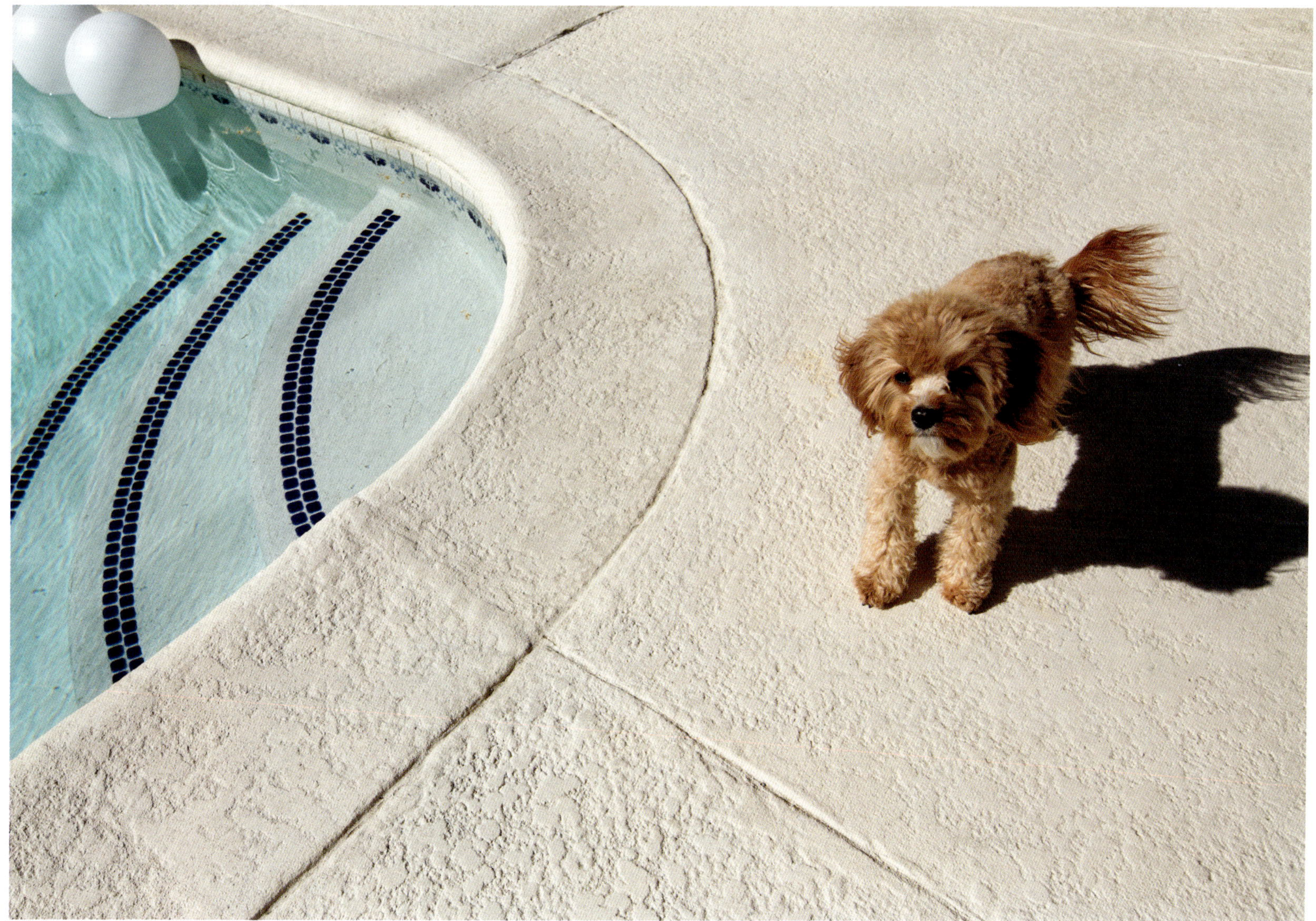

Fanny

**JACK RUSSELL
RESCUE**

ARCHITECT: JACK MEISELMAN, 1958

Our pets have been responsible for life-changing decisions we've made. Our first rescue adoption, thirty years ago, led us from an urban Lower East Side apartment in Manhattan to a home in a beach community in the Hamptons. She needed a place to run freely, and, since Linda had been rescued from Puerto Rico, she needed a beach. Fanny has led us from that same beach community to Palm Springs, since sun is her elixir, and we were more than happy to follow.

Sixty-plus years after being built, our home feels as modern today as it must have felt then. The restorative elements of the glass, the light, and the landscape influences our well-being every day—and because the Palm Springs community is so welcoming, not only to humans but to their four-legged family members, an atmosphere of positive interaction pervades here.

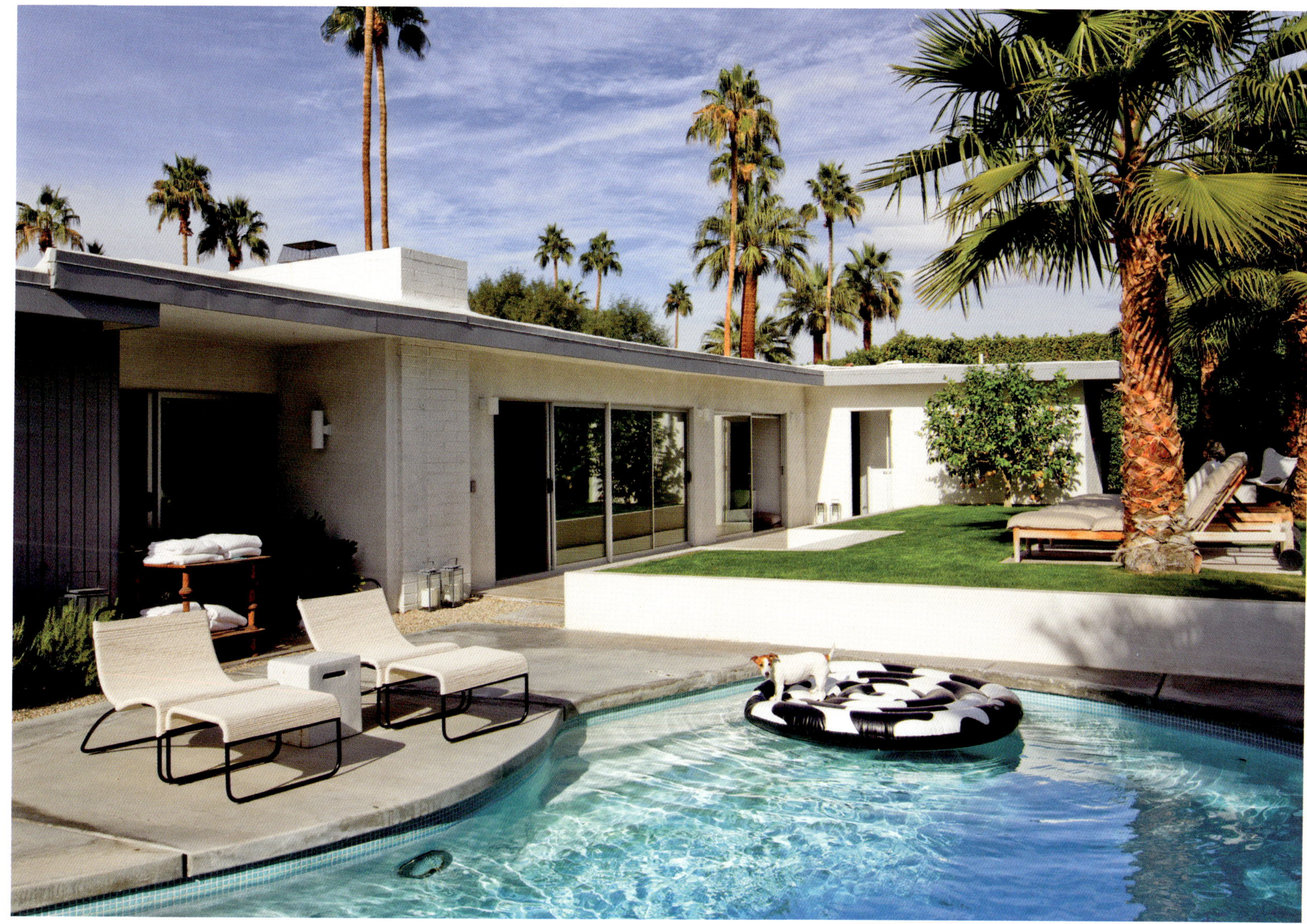

Charlie

STANDARD PARTI POODLE

ARCHITECT: WILLIAM KRISEL, 1963

It wouldn't be a home without a four-legged family member.

We always wanted to be in paradise.

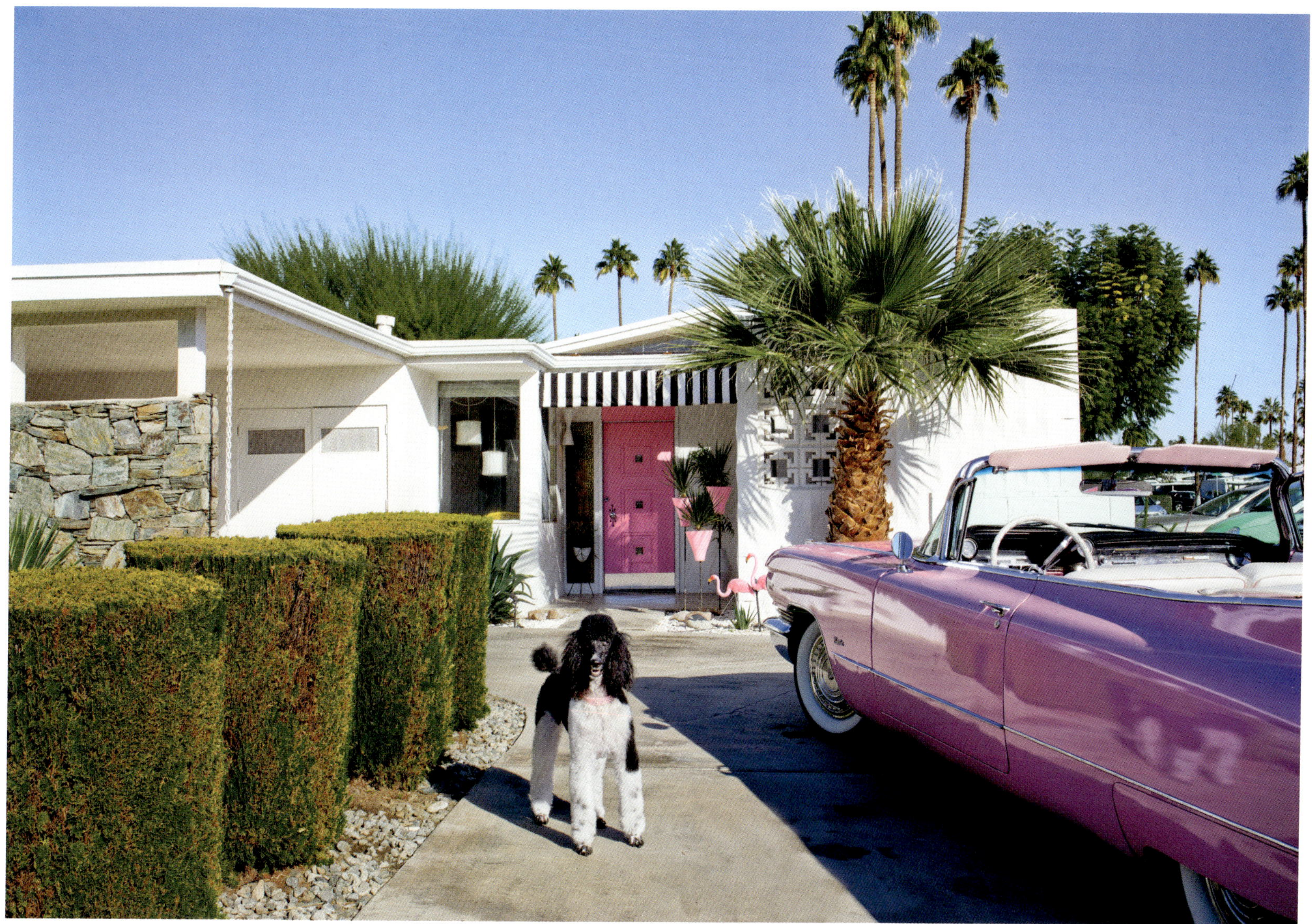

Miss Emma

**BELGIAN TERVUREN / SHEPHERD MIX
RESCUE**

TRAILER: 1956 LINCRAFT

Miss Emma is that calm, yet attentive, presence that warms our home, and when she is absent, you feel it. Ever watchful, she likes to guard the thresholds and doorways that you are near—or is it just to catch a belly rub or a few sweet words as you move through the house? I particularly like how she embraces our friends and makes them all feel like they are the only ones who can give her the love she needs. If only we could clone her. She is a cherished part of our family life.

We love our old Lincraft trailer. It serves as a bar for parties and backdrop for our everyday outdoor living—a sweet reminder that the good life is at hand.

Palm Springs itself remains a resort town, but with a lot of city conveniences for comfort. People are relaxed and citrus grows on trees here!!! Whether it's a crisp winter night and a cozy fire (and a glass of wine) is called for, or you are dining under warm starlight with bare arms, time slows down in Palm Springs. . . . Maybe it's the intoxicating perfume of jasmine and citrus blossom . . .

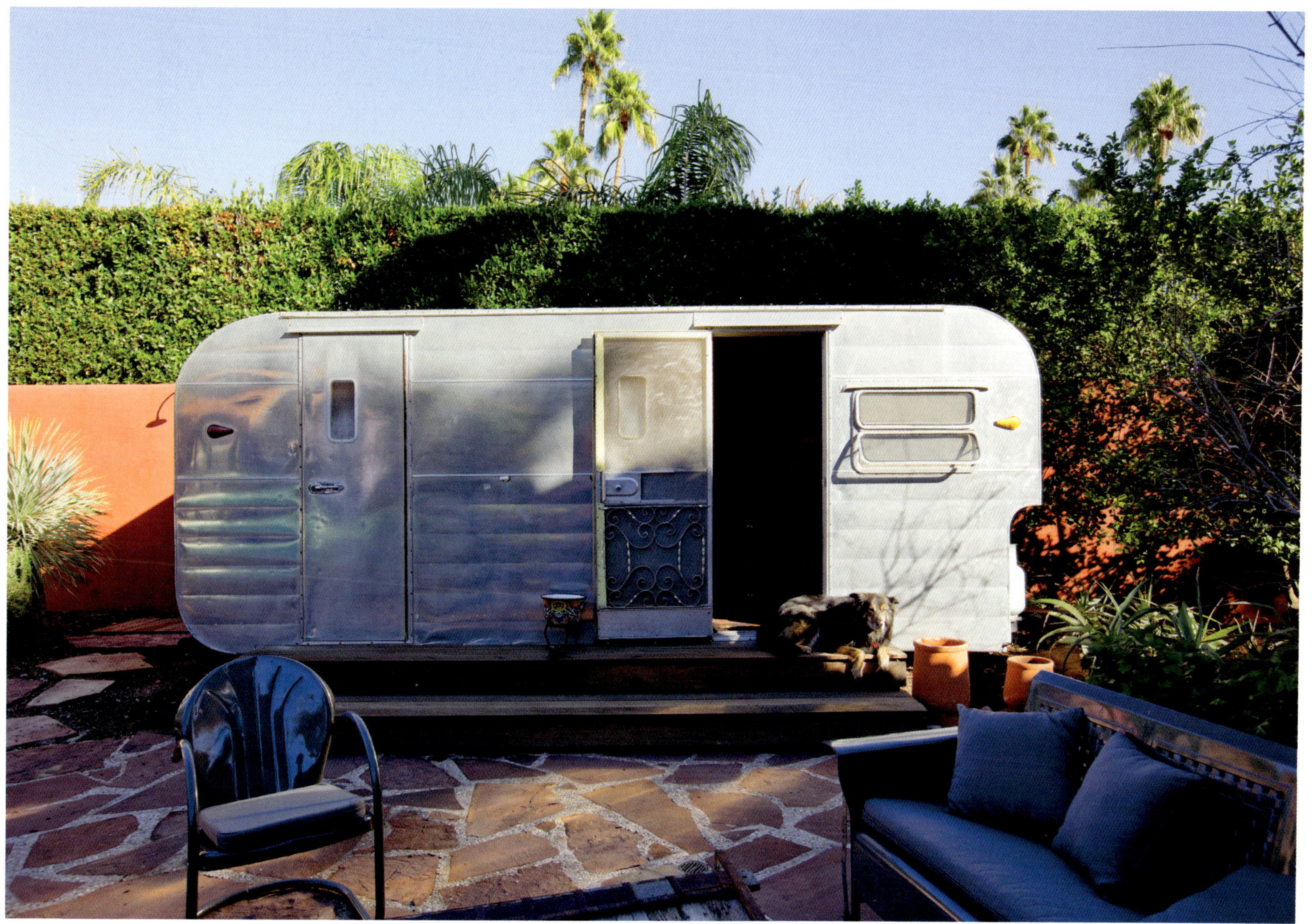

Steve

**IRISH WOLFHOUND
RESCUE**

ARCHITECT UNKNOWN, 1953

Palm Springs is a city that welcomes dogs, even one that is 165 pounds! Steve is the kindest, sweetest dog we have ever had. He loves people and enjoys going to Vintage Market and all the dog-friendly restaurants like Birba, Copley's, and 4 Paws Coffee. Everyone remembers Steve, and he has recently applied for his Palm Springs Walk of Fame Star.

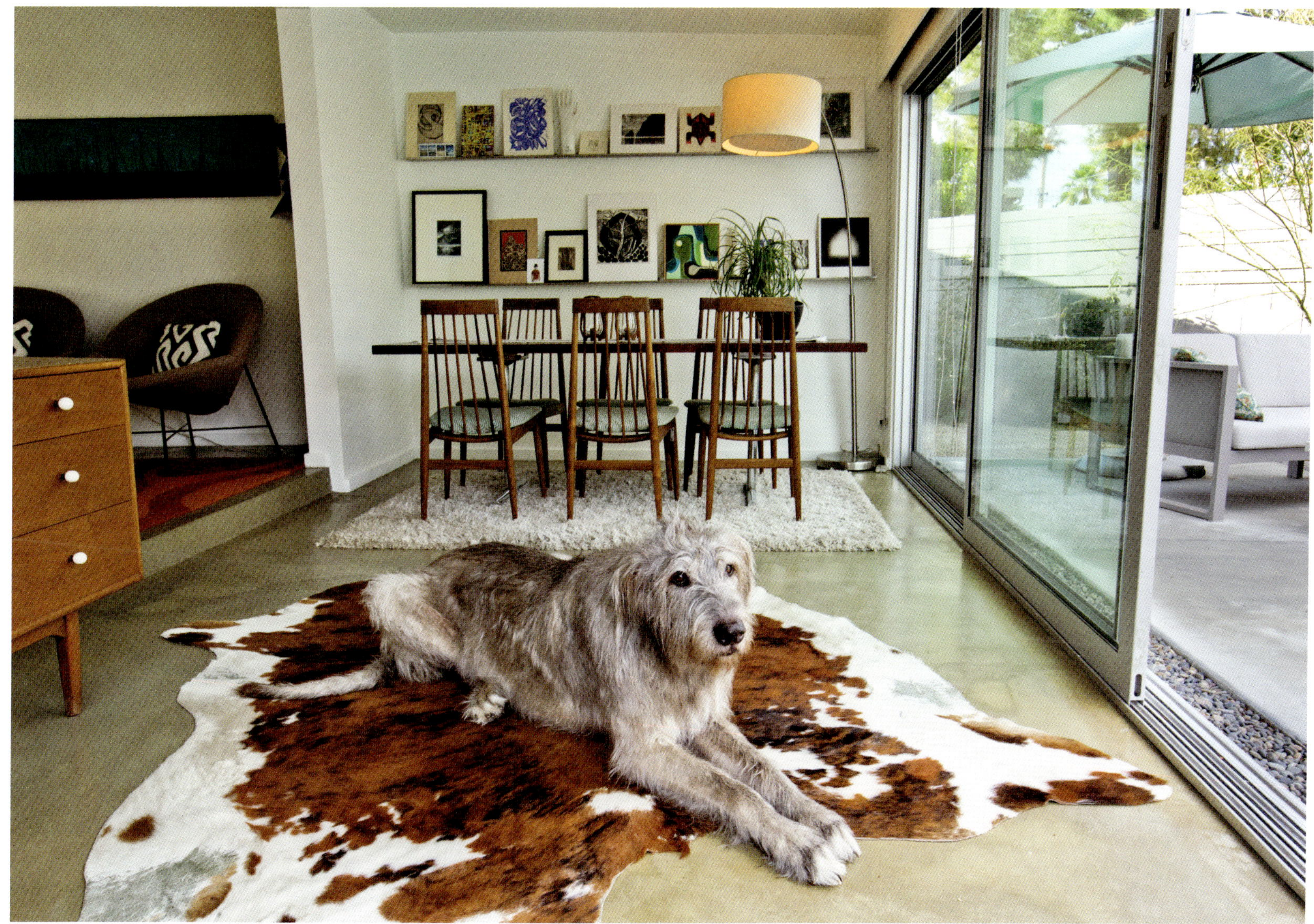

Blanquita

MIXED BREED, RESCUED FROM A BEACH IN COSTA RICA

HOME BUILT BY RYAN AND RYAN, 1955

Blanquita has been an integral part of the family for over ten years now. She brings a smile to everyone's face throughout the day. She is in tune with everyone's energy and is always ensuring, through the wag of her tail and funny little noises she makes, that everyone is happy. She is a bright light in our family!!

I love the clean lines of the midcentury modern architecture, the play of light through the clerestory windows, the natural materials, and peekaboo mountain views. Palm Springs is such a quiet and easy place to live. People are relaxed and happy, and there is a shared respect and love for design and sunshine!

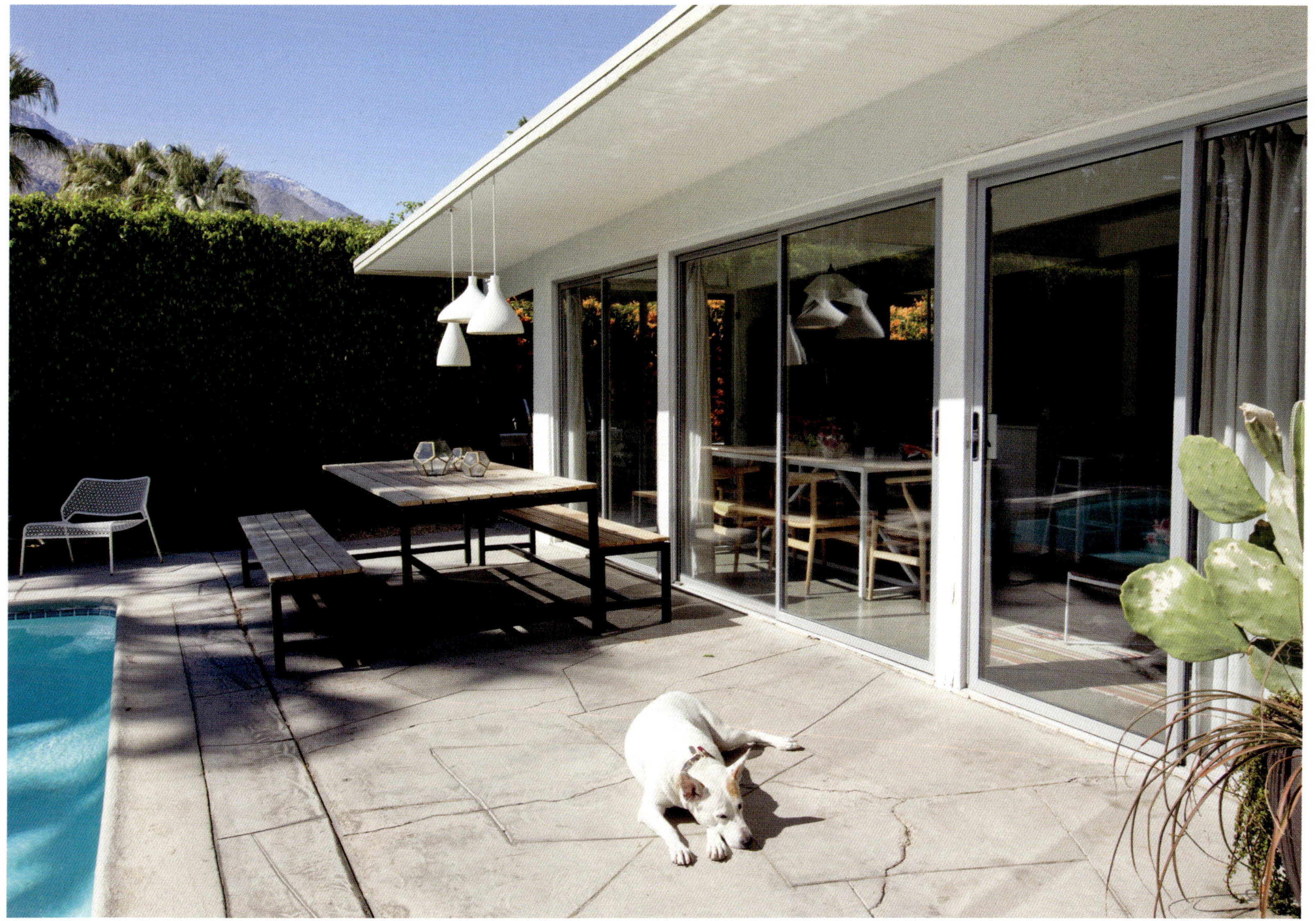

Louie

**MIXED LAB
RESCUE**

ARCHITECT: WILLIAM KRISEL, 1963

If he could, I'm sure Louie would go around singing "Forget your troubles, come on get happy!" He has an infectious joy that spreads to everyone he meets.

One of the many things that MCM homes and Palm Springs have in common is SUNSHINE! The midcentury modern aesthetic of bringing the outdoors in is perfect for this gorgeous city of Palm Springs, with its abundance of sunshine, majestic palm trees swaying gently in the breeze, and exquisite mountain views.

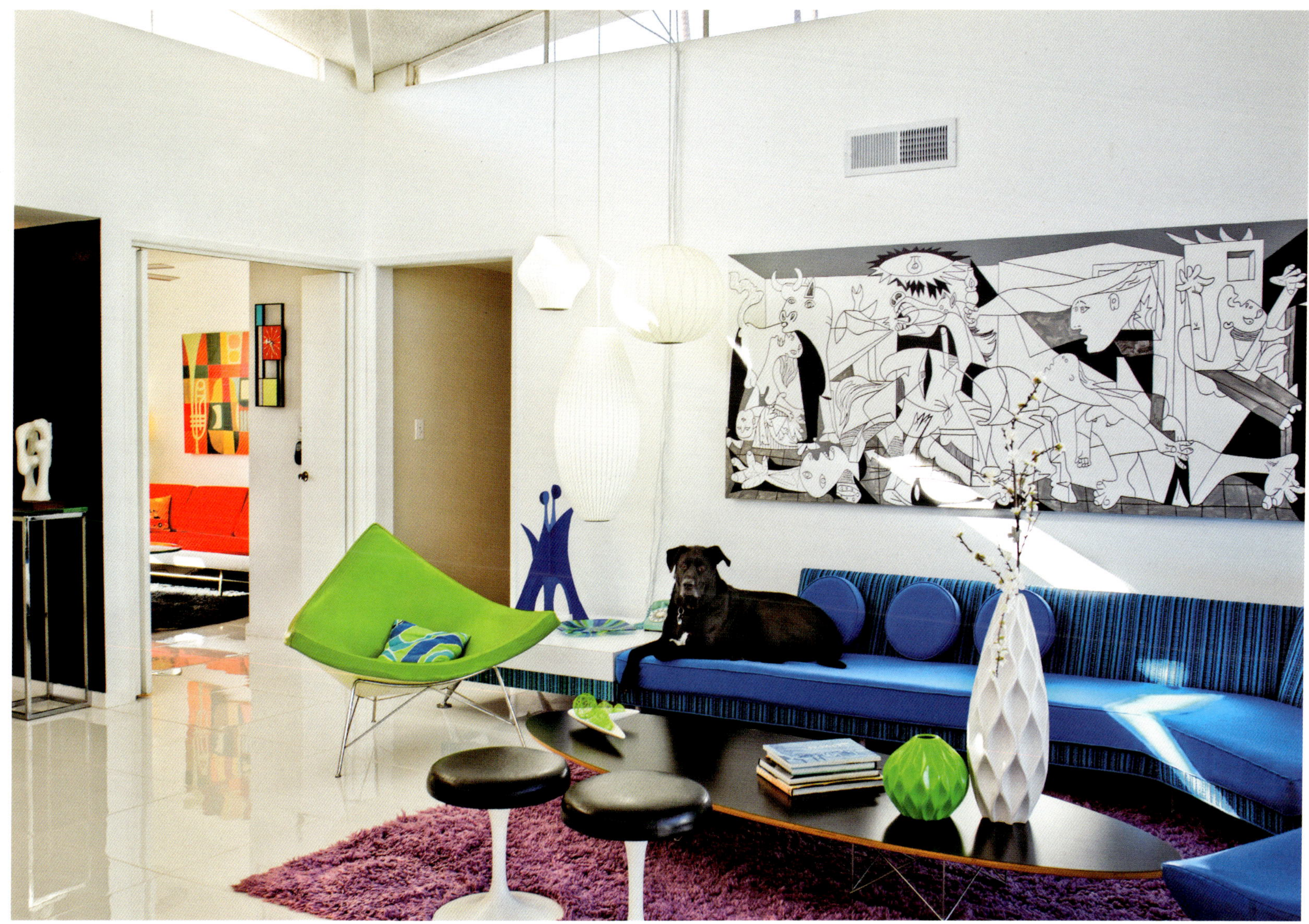

Hamilton (L) and Sydney

PARSON RUSSELL TERRIERS

ARCHITECTS: PATTEN AND WILD, 1963

It is great to arrive home after a stressful day of work and be greeted like a rock star—every time. They are warm and loving yet never cease to amuse. Their energy is contagious.

Time transcends Palm Springs. It's an escape to a life where troubles diminish, playfulness is abundant, and the enigmatic quality of the landscape never fails to delight.

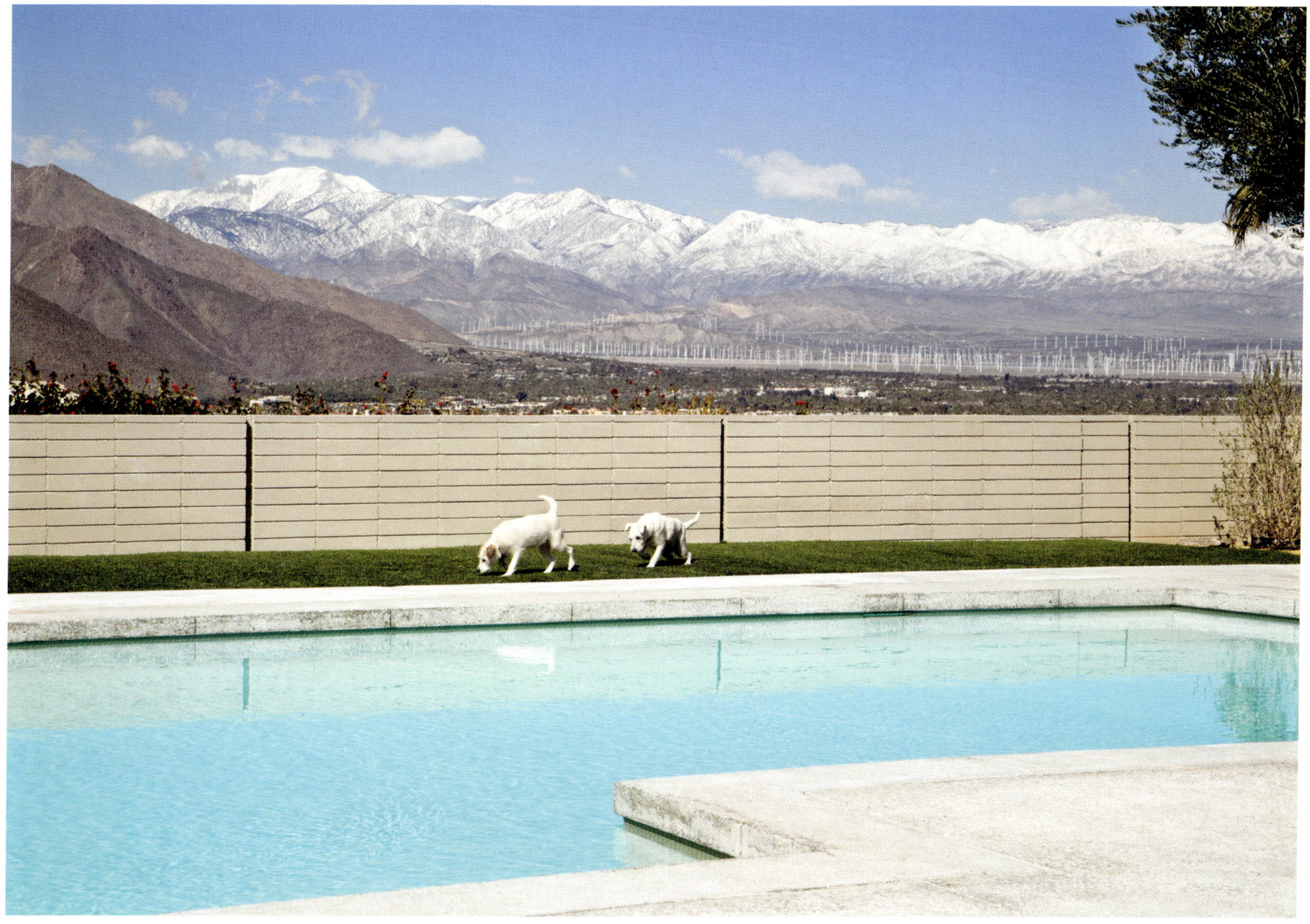

Sagan

**WHITE GERMAN SHEPHERD / HUSKY
RESCUE**

MOVIE COLONY EAST, 1963

Sagan (named for Carl Sagan) is disabled and a "senior citizen," as am I! Together we face life's challenges and revel in life's joys. His presence brings both peace and protection to our property. I'm grateful every day for his sweet companionship.

Sagan and I moved to Palm Springs to escape the harsh Minnesota weather. The climate has helped both of us be healthier and happier. Palm Springs is the ideal blend of village and world-class city. Folks are fab, and furry friends are welcome almost everywhere around town. Our Movie Colony East bungalow isn't lavish, but it's an artistic abode full of my murals and a bohemian Southwest vibe, nicknamed "HaHaHacienda." It's a little oasis for Sagan, me, and our guests—both two- and four-legged.

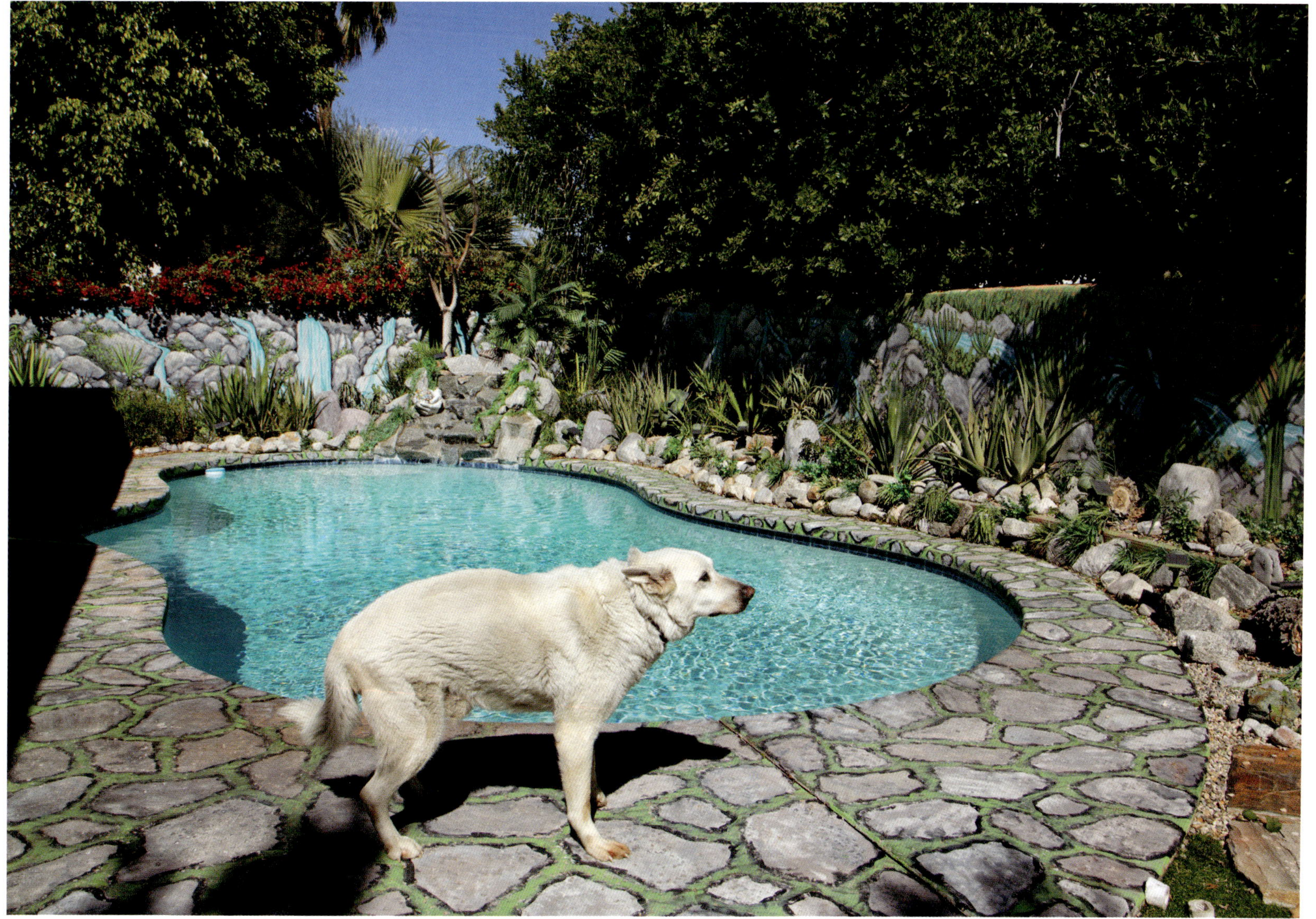

Rufus

**WHATADOODLE
RESCUE**

ESCENA GOLF CLUB, 2018

A house is a house without a pet, but a house is a home with one. Rufus is like a silent sentry, and the sounds of him padding on the carpet or clicking on the tile are a very comforting soundtrack.

There is a feeling of optimism in the architecture in Palm Springs, about positive futurism, about escaping the drab and entering the fab, about sharing and entertaining and living happily in your MCM pad. The backdrop of the mountains and the play of light that's distinct to the Coachella uniquely sets off our MCM differently than midcentury modern elsewhere—space-age design on a moonscape.

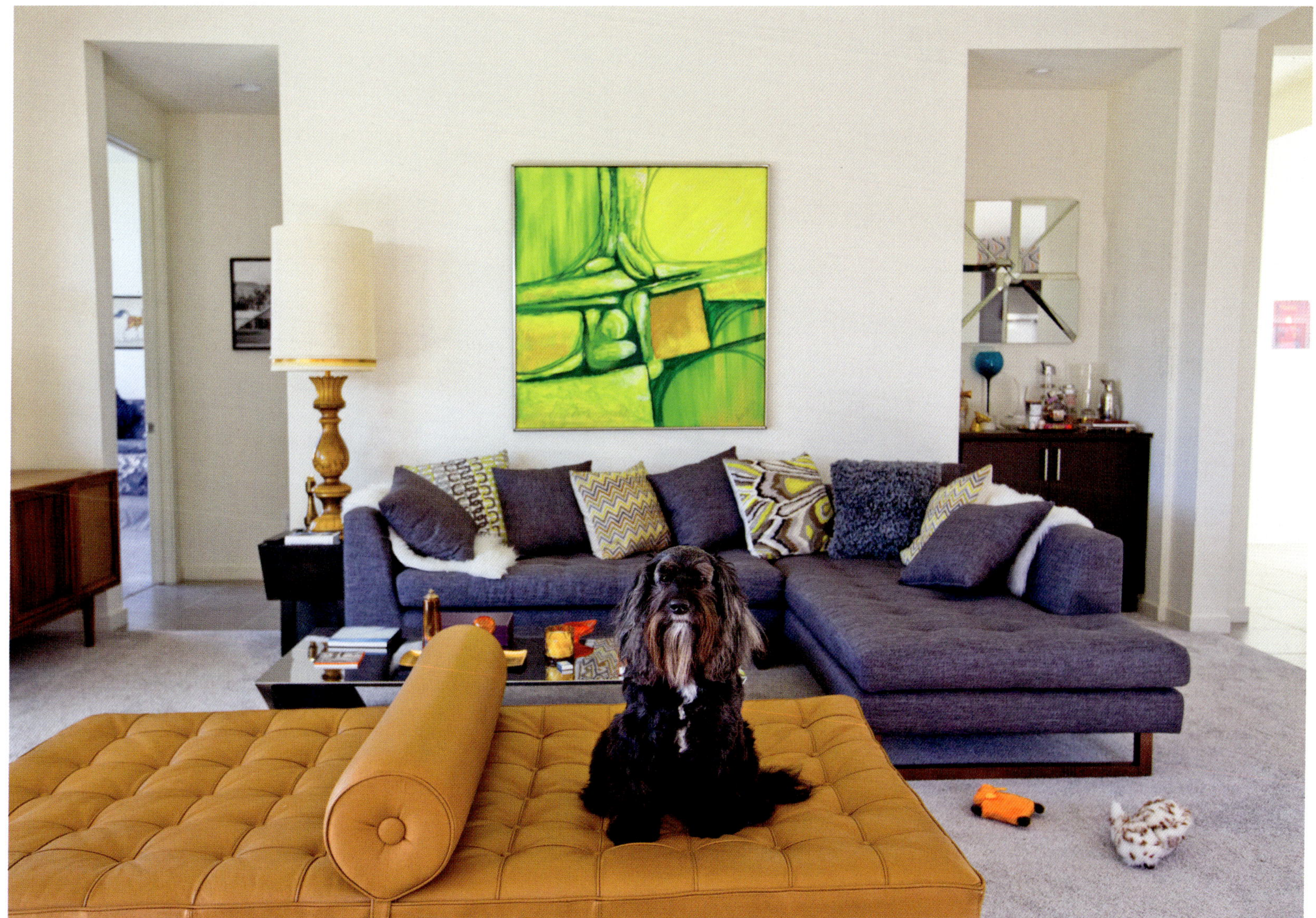

Lola

PIT BULL MIX
RESCUE

ARCHITECT: DONALD WEXLER, 1960

We moved from the cold blustery winters of Chicago four years ago and have not looked back. Lola and our mini dachshund, Arthur (see p. 32), much prefer lounging in the winter sun to the quick, snow-filled walks in Chicago. Seeing them be able to enjoy the outdoors year-round really brings a smile to our faces!

The MCM vibe is so relaxed and laid back. When we came to Palm Springs for vacation four years ago, we both fell in love with the natural beauty and laid-back lifestyle, so we packed up and made the trek cross-country to the MCM Mecca of the US.

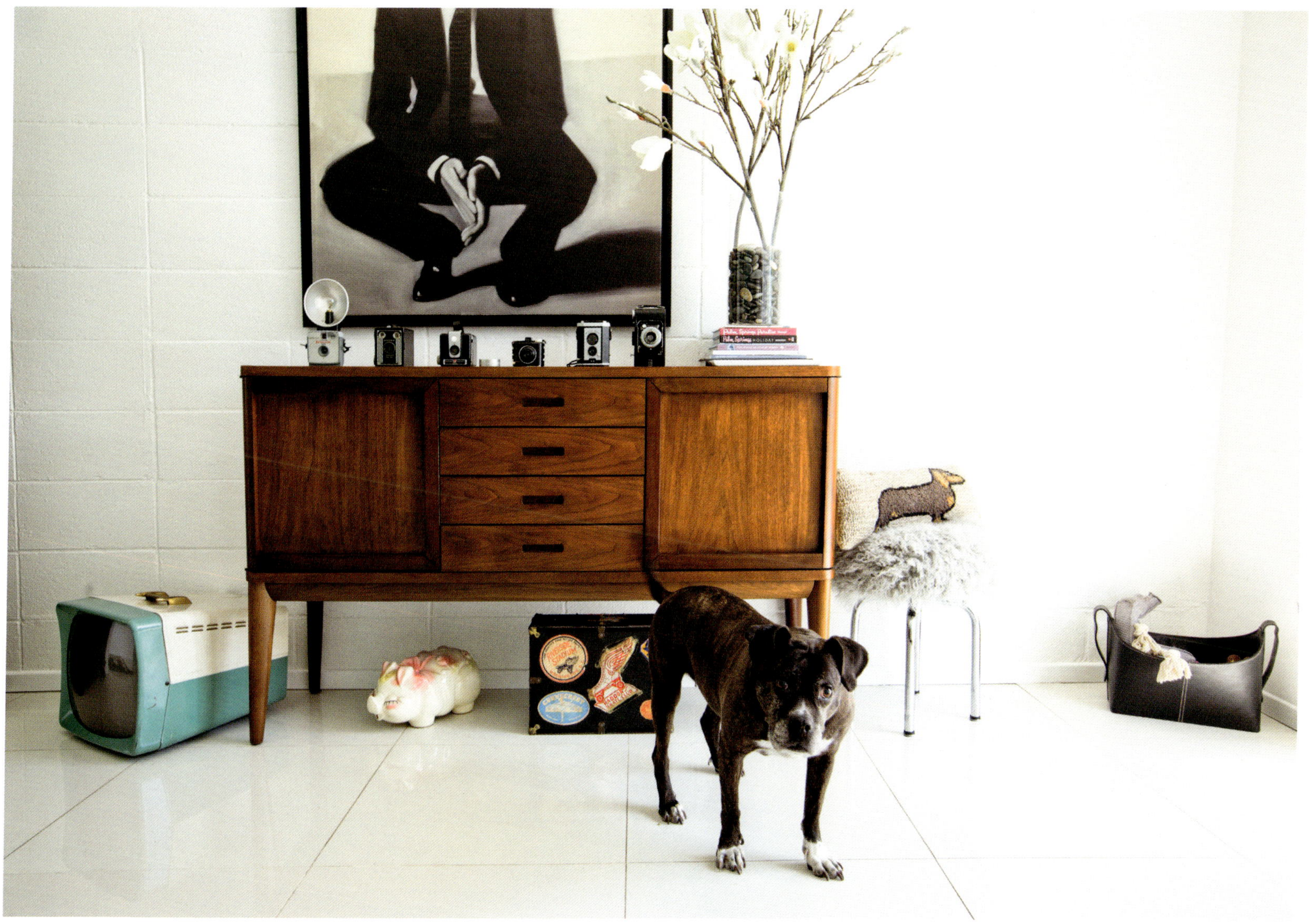

Emerson

**CAIRN TERRIER
RESCUE**

ARCHITECT: HUGH KAPTUR, 1959

Without our beloved fur babies our house was just a house; with them our house is a home.

We've spent the past eight years restoring our home rather than remodeling (or remuddling) it. We feel that we're the stewards of our home for future modernistas and have kept Kaptur's design and innovations rather than tearing out the original Pomona tiles in the kitchen and bathrooms, stainless-steel wall oven, and built-on-site cabinetry. The two greatest compliments we've gotten are that (1) Hugh Kaptur signed the inside of our coat closet (the only building of his he's ever signed), and (2) when he brought his beloved wife, Helen, to see our house shortly before she passed away, she was overwhelmed because she had never seen one of his early residences in near-original condition. As for Palm Springs, we'd never lived in such a dog-friendly town until we moved here in 2012. We're proud to be a part of the MCM brand that makes Palm Springs the epicenter of modernist design.

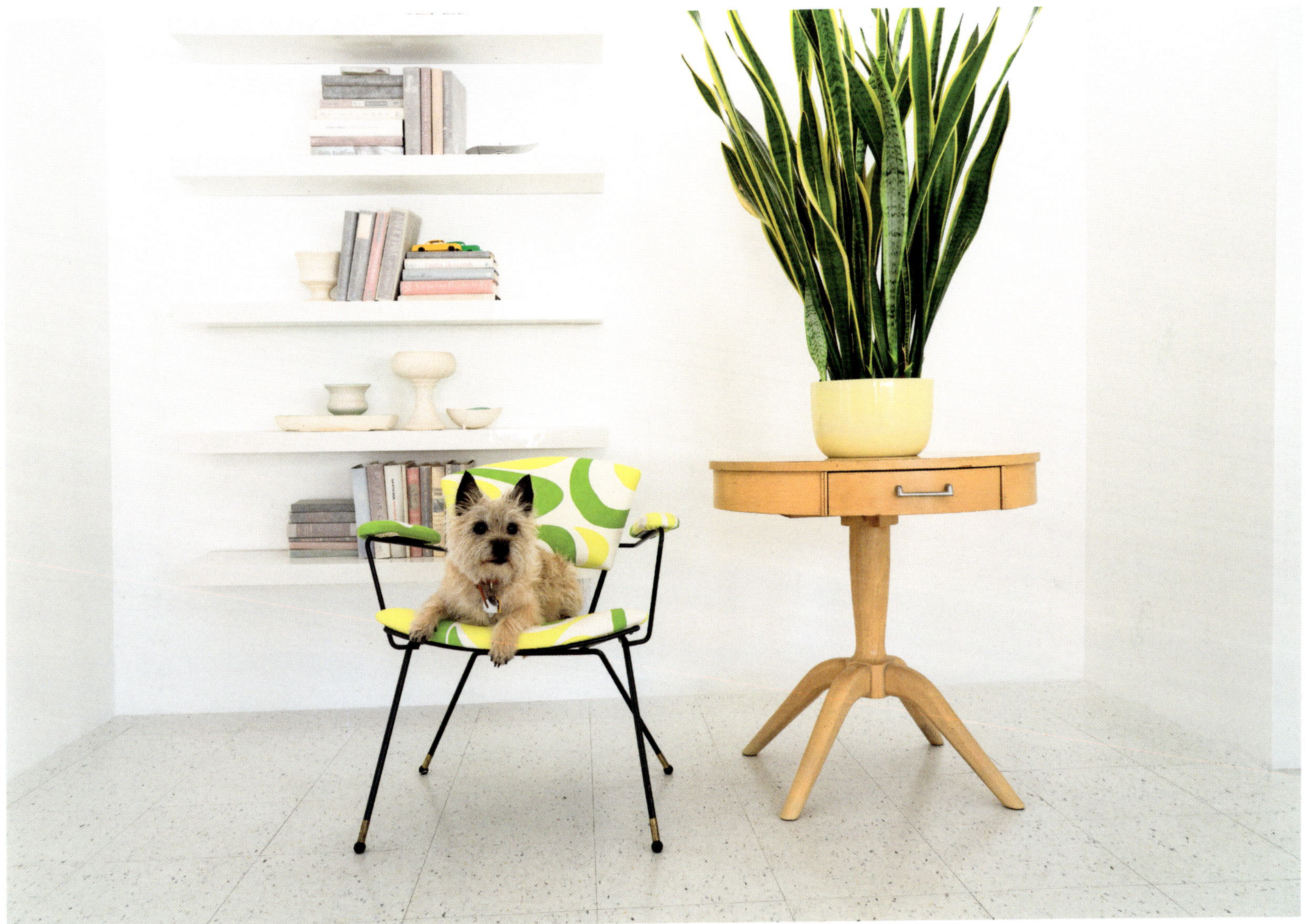

Sadie Jude

**WHEATON / AUSSIE MIX
RESCUE**

PALO FIERRO ESTATES, 1962

A wall of glass in the bedroom means that every morning, at the first light of day, Sadie becomes spring-loaded. The slightest rustle of the sheets is her signal to jump over the corners of the bed, taunting us to get up and get the day started. Anxious for our early-morning walk around our Canyon Country Club neighborhood, she's aloof with the morning regulars—more excited to find some lawn on which to nose-dive, roll on her back, and kick her legs into the air, then take a few manic and speedy orbits around us with her leash fully extended.

Once home, her bursts of high energy turn to calm as she rests her head on the cool metal base of the Saarinen Tulip side table. Under her bangs are soulful eyes—our shaggy love—she's twelve now yet has never outgrown her puppy demeanor.

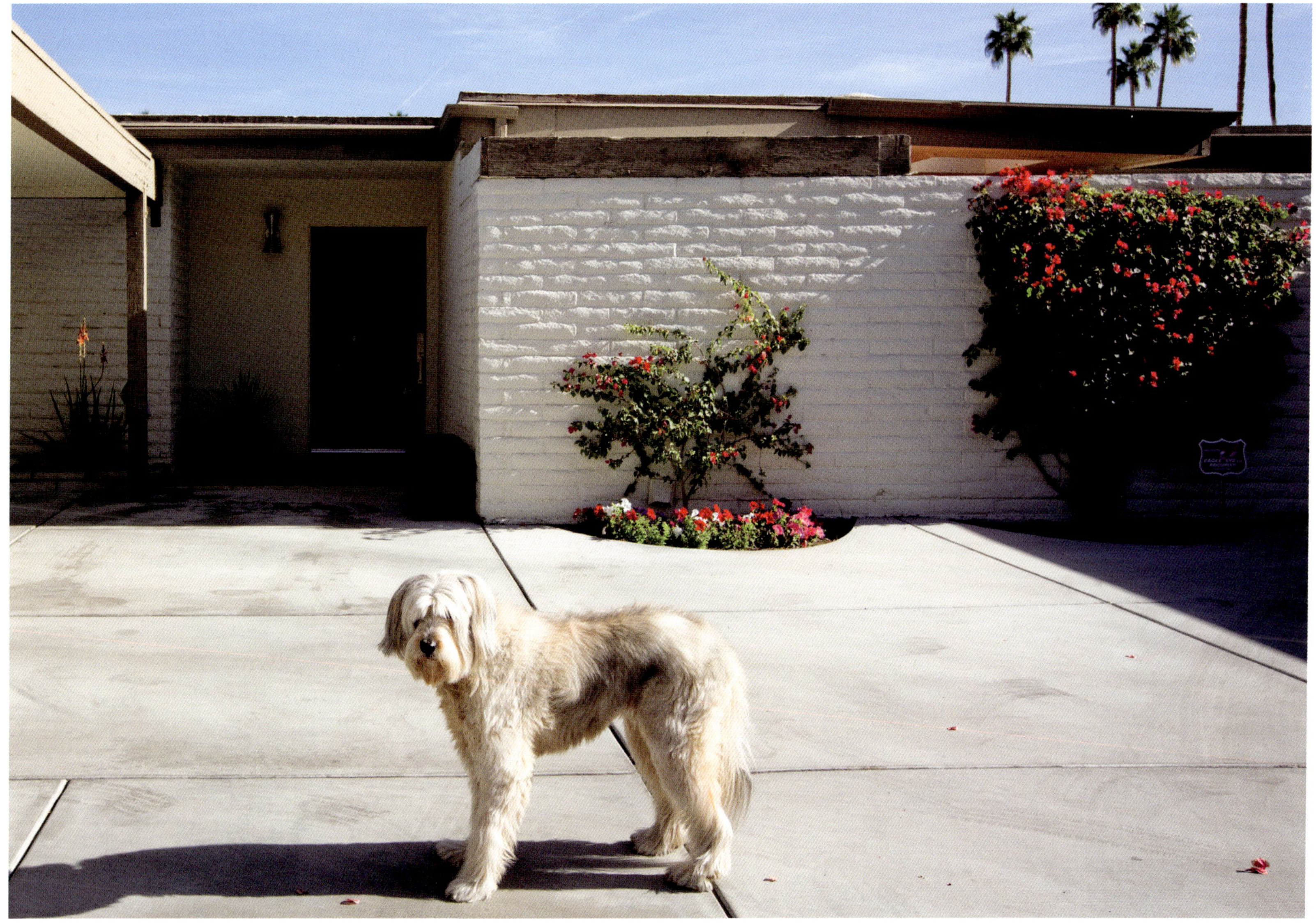

Nancy Baron

Born in Chicago, Nancy Baron is now based in Los Angeles and Palm Springs, California. Her portraits, landscapes, and architectural photographs capture the majesty of the world nearby with a hopeful bias.

Nancy's prints have been exhibited in group and solo shows internationally and are held in public and private collections. Her photography has been published in notable publications worldwide, including the *New York Times, Madame Figaro, W Magazine, Architectural Digest*, the *Telegraph Magazine, Condé Nast Traveler, Fast Times*, and *Mother Jones*, and on the Apple, CNN, and BBC websites.

Baron's two previous monographs, *The Good Life > Palm Springs* and *Palm Springs > The Good Life Goes On*, published by Kehrer Verlag, are held in various museum libraries, including MOMA, LACMA, the J. Paul Getty Museum, the Center for Documentary Studies at Duke University, and the Harry Ransom Center at the University of Texas, Austin.

Sia

Australian-born singer / songwriter / animal rights advocate Sia divides her time between Los Angeles, Palm Springs, and the world with her dogs, Lick-Lick, Pantera, and Cereal.

Bob Merlis

Splitting his time between Los Angeles and Palm Springs, Bob Merlis is an automotive journalist whose writing has been published both in general-interest and enthusiast periodicals.

Outside the field of automotive journalism and literature, Merlis continues his endeavors in the music industry, where he is best known for his almost thirty-year tenure at Warner Bros. Records, where he was senior vice president, director of worldwide corporate communications. Beyond his corporate duties, he worked as a publicist on behalf of such artists as Neil Young, Chris Isaak, Prince, Madonna, Ice-T, the Sex Pistols, Emmylou Harris, R.E.M., ZZ Top, Randy Newman, Steve Earle, and many others.

Through M.f.H., his West Coast–based public relations / marketing consultancy, Merlis has been involved in a number of diverse projects on behalf of such clients as Etta James, Experience Hendrix LLC, Keely Smith, John Fogerty, John Mellencamp, ABKCO Records (Sam Cooke, the Rolling Stones), ZZ Top, the Roy Orbison Estate, Dweezil Zappa, and Memphis Music Hall of Fame, among others.

Acknowledgments

Thank you to the modern dogs of Palm Springs and their modernists for welcoming me into their beautiful homes—and to everyone who helped me document and share this lovely side of Palm Springs life.

Joel Alverson and Michael Parkey

Margie Backaus

Fred Baron

Katie Baron and Miguel, Lucia, and Alberto Jiron

Maggie Baron

Tracy Beckmann and Danny Heller

Michael Benthall and Dana Krueger

Jeffrey Bernstein and Oscar Chamudes

Rex Bonomelli and Philip Heckman

Robert Brandt and David Howard

Jennifer Braunstein

Stella and Michael Bullock

Dick Burkett and Russ Uthe

Tyler Burton and Jeff Sarpa

Melanie Caldwell

Carlos Cardoza and Teddy Lewis

David Clark and Christopher Kennedy

Amy Cox

Grant J. Crilley

Michael DeJong and Richard Haymes

John De La Rosa and Steven Keylon

Jennifer and Alex Dethier

Tom Dolle and George Waffle

Suzanne Donaldson

P. David Ebersole and Todd Hughes

Joe Enos

Johnny Follin

Berns Fry and Ricks Lee

Sean Gaston and Jim Jewell

Cyril Gaultier and Brent Zimmerman

Jim Hanlin and William Tadlock

Gretchen Hilmers

Cody Howsman and Mark Leach

Jim Isermann

Susan Secoy Jensen and Dan Jensen

Gary Johns

Lynda Keeler and Bob Merlis

Ross Klein

Lauren LeBaron and Peter Moruzzi

David A. Lee and Daniel Vaillancourt

Mark Lindal

Martin Lowery and Jade Thomas Nelson

Kali Malinka

Liz and Frank Malinka

Sherry Marks and William Shpall

Chris Menrad

J. Chris Mobley

Daryle Morgan and Dean Williams

Laura Morton and Jeff Dunas

Joseph Peterbilt and Bill Stewart

Matthew Reader

David Salyer and Barry Solof

Suzanne Shpall

Sia

Lauri Svedberg, Svedberg Studio Palm Springs

Cindra and Scott Syverson

Javier Valenzuela

Gerry Wendel

Mary and Gary Wexler

Mr. and Mrs. Woods

Kim and Joe Zakowski